Pete Maidment has been th[...] of Winchester since 2005. [...] church in Southampton and [...] with Youth for Christ in Roch[...] was in charge of a youth centre in Woking for Surrey County Council. A published author, Pete co-wrote *Reconnecting with Confirmation* (2011) and contributed to *Young People and Worship* (2007), both published by Church House Publishing. He is married and has two children.

The Rt Revd Paul Butler is Bishop of Southwell and Nottingham, and is also Advocate for Children among the Church of England bishops. He loves leading confirmation services. His previous books include *Temptation and Testing* (SPCK, 2007), and *Reaching Children* (1992) and *Reaching Families* (1995), both published by Scripture Union. He contributed to *Through the Eyes of a Child* (Church House Publishing, 2009) and *Reconnecting with Confirmation*. He is married to Rosemary and they have four adult children.

For Dominic (aka Baby Nomnic)

and

To all young people willing to stand publicly for Jesus

LIVING YOUR CONFIRMATION

PUTTING PROMISES INTO ACTION

PETE MAIDMENT
AND
PAUL BUTLER

First published in Great Britain in 2012

Society for Promoting Christian Knowledge
36 Causton Street, London SW1P 4ST
www.spckpublishing.co.uk

British Library Cataloguing-in-Publication Data
A catalogue record for this book is available from the British Library

ISBN 978-0-281-06462-5
eBook ISBN 978-0-281-06761-9

10 9 8 7 6 5 4 3 2 1

Designed and typeset by Penguin Boy Ltd (www.penguinboy.net)
First printed in Great Britain by Ashford Colour Press

Produced on paper from sustainable forests

CONTENTS

ACKNOWLEDGEMENTS

Writing *Living Your Confirmation* has been great fun and a real challenge. I'm especially grateful to Matthew Fewtrell, Judith Moore, Emily Saunders and Jake Sudworth for taking the time to read through the book as it neared completion and for giving me such good advice. Thanks to Bishop Paul for making time in his incredibly busy schedule to provide wise words for the opening of each chapter and, of course, to Tracey Messenger from SPCK for her patience and encouragement. I'm excited to think that one day my children, Molly and Joshua, might be preparing for confirmation themselves – I am so looking forward to travelling the journey with you both as you explore the Christian faith for yourselves. Finally, I am so grateful to Kathryn for her love and support in all that I do.

Pete Maidment

INTRODUCTION

Congratulations!

You've been confirmed, and we want to join with the rest of the Church in celebrating with you what an amazing achievement that is!

You may not even have realized yet just what you've done. Confirmation is a really big deal – standing up in front of your church, your friends and your family and declaring publicly, maybe for the first time, what it means for you to be a Christian. We hope that you've kept a copy of the order of service and that if you received any gifts they're in a safe place. We want you to remember the day of your confirmation for the rest of your life – confirmation is something to be really proud of and to celebrate!

We're sure you realize that getting confirmed isn't the end of a journey. It may feel like your confirmation preparation was getting you ready for an exam and that the service was like sitting the paper at the end of the course. The early Christians described their faith as 'The Way'. For them, being a Christian was more than a lifestyle choice or a recreational activity – it was a way of life. The Way could also describe a journey, and for many Christians that's what life and the Christian faith is like. Confirmation is another step on that journey – it's neither the start nor the end. Loads of young people use those kinds of words to describe what confirmation meant to them.

That's why this book is called *Living Your Confirmation*. It's designed to help you to carry on in that journey, to live out many of the things that you said or that were said over you in the service. Our hope is that in these pages you'll be reminded of your confirmation service, and you'll find tools and ideas to help you put into practice some of the things you promised. We hope you'll find it thought-provoking and challenging and that you'll find plenty of practical things to help you on your way.

Each chapter of the book takes a sentence or part of a sentence from the 'Commission' part of the Confirmation service, and unpacks it (the Commission is printed in full on page 3). Each chapter begins with a reflection from Paul Butler, the Bishop of Southwell and Nottingham. He'll help you understand why the sentence is in the service and what it means for him to say it as he confirms people. There'll be a Bible verse that backs up each promise or sentence, and a reflection on what it means and how to keep on living it. Each section also contains a chance to 'reflect' and 'react'.

The 'Reflect' section is a chance for you to spend some time in quiet thinking about what you've read and in working out what it might mean for you day-by-day as you carry on in your faith. The 'React' section will give you some kind of activity to help you get out there and live your faith in the real world.

Our hope is that you'll find this book helpful; that it will bring the confirmation service alive for you and help you to keep going when continuing on the Way gets tough.

For more resources, visit our website:
www.livingyourconfirmation.co.uk

Pete Maidment and Bishop Paul Butler

THE COMMISSION
(FROM THE CONFIRMATION SERVICE)

Those who are baptized are called to worship and serve God.

*Will you continue in the apostles' teaching and fellowship,
in the breaking of bread, and in the prayers?*
With the help of God, I will.

*Will you persevere in resisting evil,
and, whenever you fall into sin, repent and return to the Lord?*
With the help of God, I will.

*Will you proclaim by word and example
the good news of God in Christ?*
With the help of God, I will.

*Will you seek and serve Christ in all people,
loving your neighbour as yourself?*
With the help of God, I will.

*Will you acknowledge Christ's authority over human society,
by prayer for the world and its leaders,
by defending the weak, and by seeking peace and justice?*
With the help of God, I will.

*May Christ dwell in your hearts through faith,
that you may be rooted and grounded in love
and bring forth the fruit of the Spirit.*
Amen. [1]

'GOD HAS CALLED YOU BY NAME':
WHAT CONFIRMATION IS ALL ABOUT
BISHOP PAUL BUTLER

**'GOD HAS CALLED YOU BY NAME AND MADE YOU HIS OWN.
CONFIRM, O LORD, YOUR SERVANT WITH YOUR HOLY SPIRIT.'**

This is the point that you may well remember most in your confirmation, for it's when you were alone with God and the bishop, even if physically surrounded by others. It's the central act in the whole Confirmation service.

I love this moment for each person I confirm. It's an enormous privilege (and responsibility). I know how important it is to each individual, of whatever age. I know that in some way God is meeting with that person. So when you were confirmed by your bishop, I know it was important to you and that God was at work in you at that moment. Let me explore this a little more with you as we begin this book.

'God has called you by name and made you his own.' The prophet Isaiah said to the people of Israel, 'I have called you by name, you are mine' (Isaiah 43.1 ESV). This was to assure them together of God's love, call, and that they really belonged to him.

Jesus said this:

He who enters by the door is the shepherd of the sheep . . . The sheep hear his voice, and he calls his own sheep by name and leads them out. When he has brought out all his own, he goes before them, and the sheep follow him, for they know his voice . . . I am the good shepherd. The good shepherd lays down his life for the sheep . . . I am the good shepherd. I know my own and my own know me.   (John 10.1–15 ESV)

Your parent(s) are likely to have taken a lot of time and trouble in deciding on your name. Very few parents just randomly pick a name for their child. They want it to be one that they like, that has some family significance or even some meaning. In many parts of the world children have several names that they're given because of the meaning. So Ugandan friends of mine named their first child Blessings because they saw him as a great blessing from God; their later children are named Hope, Faith, Timothy and Titus because of the importance of these in the Bible. A Nigerian friend is called Sunday, both because he was born on a Sunday and because it's the day of resurrection.

My parents called me Paul mainly because they liked the name. But for me it's also been important that I bear the name of St Paul. When I learnt the story of Paul's conversion and how he was originally called Saul, I was fascinated by the fact that Saul means 'great' while Paul means 'small'. God deliberately changes his name to remind him of his small, humble place rather than his earlier arrogant sense of greatness. My surname is Butler. This must mean that a long way back in time my ancestors worked as butlers, that is, as wine waiters or servants. I like the fact that my name means 'small servant'; for me it's a great reminder of one aspect of what God calls me to be.

Our names matter – our identity is tied up with our name; this is how we're recognized and known. Well, God calls and knows us by name. He knows you personally. He loves you as you, not as someone else, not simply as part of the mass of humanity. He knows and loves you as an individual. This is why that moment at your confirmation was so special. It was a clear reminder that God knows and calls you by name.

Why not take a moment to think about this now? Quietly say to yourself something like: 'God has called me by name; he knows me as [insert your name]; he loves me as [insert your name]'. Thank God for this wonderful truth.

So this was at the heart of your confirmation service. Let's take a short while to reflect on what else was happening.

For a start you were *doing* something. You were confirming your own faith in Jesus Christ as Lord. You did this openly and publicly in front of family, friends and the assembled congregation. It was a bold step. You did it simply by being there. You did it in the part of the service called the Decision. Here you confirmed your own commitment to the promises that were made for you by parents and godparents at your baptism (if you were baptized as a baby or young child) or by you at your own baptism (if this happened at a separate occasion from your confirmation). So you affirmed with your own mouth your personal repentance (turning away from sin and wrongdoing) and your commitment to accept and follow Jesus Christ as Lord (boss) and Saviour (deliverer or rescuer).

Then, joined by the congregation, you also affirmed your belief in the Christian faith outlined in the creed. This is called the Profession of Faith. You may well have symbolically recognized this by either signing yourself with water from the baptism font or being sprinkled with water from there by the bishop.

So by confirming your own faith in these ways you also recognized that you're part of the whole family of God, the Church. You confirmed your commitment not only to Jesus Christ but to your fellow followers of Jesus.

But when it came to the act of confirmation, first the bishop prayed over you, then he might have anointed you with oil and laid his hands on you. Here the emphasis was on God confirming you. God was confirming that he knows you by name. God was confirming his love for you and acceptance of you in Jesus Christ.

This confirming of you by God has a great deal to do with the Holy Spirit. Now the Holy Spirit has been at work in you all the way through. It's the Holy Spirit who helps us see God for who he truly is in Jesus Christ. It's the Holy Spirit who convicts us of our sin and need for repentance and forgiveness. It's the Holy Spirit who gives us faith and brings us into new life in Christ. It's the Holy Spirit who baptizes us into being members of the body of Christ. It's the Holy Spirit who helps us live the Christian life. But in the act of confirmation, God confirms us in the life of the Spirit by strengthening us afresh.

The bishop's prayer is based on Isaiah 11.2–3. These verses speak about the Messiah, that is, Jesus himself. But in the act of confirmation the bishop prays that these same gifts of the Holy Spirit will be real in your life as well: wisdom, understanding, counsel, strength, knowledge, the fear of the Lord (this is not being afraid of the Lord but being awed and amazed by his greatness and holiness). Then in the act of anointing with oil (symbolizing the Holy Spirit), the laying on of hands and the prayer 'Confirm, O Lord, your servant with your Holy Spirit', God met with you to confirm and strengthen you in your commitment to follow

'GOD HAS CALLED YOU BY NAME'

Jesus Christ and serve God as part of his Church in the future. Some people are even physically aware of God meeting them at this point; others feel nothing – but either way, God always keeps his promise, and he strengthened you and is committed to continuing to do so for the rest of your life. God is not going to let go of you – he loves you too much to do that.

So the question that then arises is, 'What next?' This is why the Commission takes place. The Commission spells out what it means to follow Jesus Christ and serve him in the world. In responding to the bishop's questions, you recognized that you need God's help every moment of every day to live a life like Jesus. You also promised with that help to live this new life. 'With the help of God, I will.'

That's what this book is all about. Each chapter will recall one part of that Commission. At the start of each chapter I'll briefly outline something of what those words mean to me whenever I read them out to those who've just been confirmed. Then Pete explores just what that might mean in our lives and offers lots of ideas to help us keep to our promise: 'With the help of God, I will.'

Please don't think Pete or I have got it all sorted – we haven't. This is why every time I ask the questions during a confirmation service I also answer them myself. I need to keep on following Jesus and I need God's help every day, just like you. The amazing and wonderful thing is that God keeps his promise and keeps strengthening and helping me – and I know he'll do the same for you.

CHAPTER 1

THE APOSTLES' TEACHING

DO YOU REMEMBER WHEN...
...YOU SAID YOU WOULD CONTINUE IN THE APOSTLES' TEACHING?

THE APOSTLES' TEACHING

BISHOP PAUL:

In a nutshell, 'the apostles' teaching' is what we find in the Bible. The apostles were the Twelve who'd been with Jesus throughout his public ministry and were witnesses to the resurrection. Alongside them Paul was added. For Jesus and the apostles, what we call the Old Testament was their 'Bible'. They valued it enormously, so we need to follow their example. The apostles passed on the story of Jesus' teaching, ministry, death and resurrection to the early Church and explained what it meant. In the end this became the Gospels, Letters and other books of what we now call the New Testament.

Throughout the Church's history, people have helped us to understand the Bible, so what others say and think about it is very important. But there's no substitute for reading and studying the Bible itself. So I think reading a small part of the Bible every day, and thinking about it, is really valuable. I also think that meeting with other Christians to study the Bible together, and learning from one another how the apostles' teaching should shape the way we live, is vital. Listening to good preaching is worth doing as well. The important thing is that we don't just get to know the Bible better in our heads but that we live our lives by its teaching because that's how we can become more and more like Jesus.

OPENER

I think it's really difficult for us in the twenty-first century to understand just how precious the Scriptures were to people in Jesus' day.

The problem we have today is that we're surrounded by so much information all the time. There's always stuff to read – books, magazines and newspapers are printed at a faster rate than ever before and the TV is constantly throwing new stuff at us. If you're like me then you probably read hundreds of snippets of information every day, just by checking up on your Facebook or Twitter account. I'm constantly bombarded by friends telling me what they've been up to today or what they think about certain subjects.

> LET THE MESSAGE OF CHRIST DWELL AMONG YOU RICHLY AS YOU TEACH AND ADMONISH ONE ANOTHER WITH ALL WISDOM THROUGH PSALMS, HYMNS, AND SONGS FROM THE SPIRIT, SINGING TO GOD WITH GRATITUDE IN YOUR HEARTS.
> (COLOSSIANS 3.16 NIV)

It's hard for us to imagine a time when information was very rare. For Jesus and the people of his time, what we call the Old Testament – and what he called the Law of Moses, the Prophets and Psalms or simply the Scriptures – was one of the few pieces of writing available. It was treated with real respect because it was understood to be God's word for his people. It's likely that by the time he was a teenager, Jesus and others his age would have learnt whole sections of the Scriptures by heart.

THE APOSTLES' TEACHING

People sometimes refer to one of the Psalms that describes God's words as sweet to the taste, '. . . sweeter than honey to my mouth!' (Psalm 119.103 NIV). They say that when a teacher – or rabbi – first sat down with his class of children, he'd produce a jar of rare and expensive honey and give each of the children some to eat. Then he'd read these verses to them. The rabbi wanted his students to realize just how amazing God's word is, how the Scriptures are sweet and rare and precious.

For most of us, the way we most regularly engage with the Bible will be at church or in a youth group. Being part of a group or congregation, and listening to the Bible being read and then to someone speaking about the meaning the words, has been a central part of the Church since the very first days of the Christian faith. In Jesus' time and right up to the invention of the printing press, listening to someone reading the Scriptures would have been the only access ordinary people had to the Word of God. Being part of a community that listens to God's word, preached or read from the Bible, is still a key part of doing church.

Bible studies in our youth group or small group or in a house group are also great ways to engage with Scripture. I love it when I read a passage to my youth group on a Sunday morning and then ask them what they think the passage is about. I learn so much from their thoughts and reflections because hearing someone else's perspective on a passage can reveal things to us that we'd never have noticed by ourselves.

Lots of Christians, however, would say that no matter how good your small group is or how amazing the sermons at your church, there's no substitute for finding time to read the Bible for yourself.

The thought of learning whole sections of Scripture by heart as Jesus would have done might be quite daunting. If we're honest, lots of us struggle to read even a verse a day. In fact for some of us reading the Bible on our own might be something completely alien – we may be used to hearing it read at church, but the thought of opening the Bible at home and reading it for our own benefit might be simply outside our experience.

If you were setting out on a long journey, maybe a long walk for a Duke of Edinburgh expedition, then you'd never set out without eating first. You need energy for the journey and you need to eat more as you travel in order to keep your strength up. It's much the same for your Christian journey: in order to grow as Christians, in order to make those promises we made at Confirmation a reality, we really need to feed ourselves. We need that sweet honey. We need to engage with the Bible.

I wonder why so many of us find this difficult. One reason might be that we often find the Bible quite hard to understand. We're used to reading things quickly, skimming our way through a novel or letting our eyes skip over a Facebook page to see if anything interesting jumps out. The Bible needs to be read differently. If you've studied English literature at school, you'll know that your teacher will be able to draw masses of detail from what seem like the simplest words or phrases. If we want to get the best out of the Bible, we need to read it with that kind of attention – and when life is so busy, that can seem like a real drag.

The most important thing about reading the Bible is that you need to remember that it's more than a dusty book (or, to be accurate, a collection of books) full of dead words. It might best be described as a living book. It's not like a novel, where you can let the words drift into your head and out again. You can't just think, 'Oh, that was nice', and move on.

The Bible, read well, will change your life. Some bits will jump out and grab your attention, some will seem shocking or surprising, and others will seem confusing and contradictory. It's a living text, and sometimes you have to let it lead you.

It's also worth being aware that there are loads of different versions of the Bible. Over the centuries people have translated and retranslated the Bible to try to get an accurate version of the originals. While it's true that scholars might think one translation is better than another, it's really best just to try to find one that you enjoy reading and are comfortable with. Why not ask your vicar or youth leader what they would recommend?

WAYS OF READING THE BIBLE

When we just skim the Bible we often miss bits because our mind is off in other places. Or sometimes there's just so much going on in the passage that we miss some of the finer points. There are lots of ways of reading the Bible that might help you avoid these kinds of distractions.

Many people use daily Bible notes that suggest a passage to read each day and give you some thoughts on what the text might mean and how to apply it to your life. Some people read daily notes printed in a book or magazine, or might have regular emails or podcasts that they follow (WordLive is a good example from Scripture Union). There are even Bible-reading programs you can download to a smartphone (YouVersion is definitely worth a look). Other people like to try to read the whole Bible in a year, and so will follow a plan that gives them a few passages to read each day to help them get through. You might want to try a Bible-memorizing activity, such as flashcards that have just one verse on for each day that you can say to yourself over and again to try to commit the words to heart. Some churches will have a daily 'service of the word' where, following a text called the 'Lectionary', they'll read portions of the Bible every day. I'll share some specific publications and resources that you might find helpful in the 'React' section at the end of this chapter.

For me, one of the best ways to get the most out of the Bible is to do something called Lectio Divina. Lectio Divina is a Latin phrase that means holy or divine reading. In the fourth and fifth centuries, St Benedict founded a community for monks in Italy. The Benedictines, as these monks became known, followed Benedict's writings, or 'rules', which included the instruction to read the Bible in this very special way.

Lectio Divina is a way of reading the Bible simply and slowly that helps us to get the most out of it, allowing God to show us things that we may never have heard of before, or may have missed. Read on to discover more about it.

REFLECT

Lectio Divina is a great way to read the Bible, but it's important to prepare yourself first. It's not like picking up a magazine or a novel and just plunging in for a few pages. Reading the Bible is a way to hear God speaking, and when you're setting yourself up for that, you need to get into the right frame of mind.

THE APOSTLES' TEACHING

First of all get everything ready. Find your Bible and the passage you want to read, using one of the methods suggested above (Bible notes or a Bible-in-a-year scheme, for instance), and then sit yourself down somewhere comfortable where you're unlikely to be disturbed (and won't fall asleep!). If you want to have a go, try looking up Psalm 119.89–112. It contains that bit about the words of God being sweet like honey.

Then spend a few moments – maybe a minute or two – sitting quietly. Try focusing on your breathing. When you breathe in you take clean oxygen into your body; when you breathe out you're getting rid of all the dirty old air. Imagine that you're breathing in God and breathing out all of your worries and stresses, even just for a short while.

Once you feel relaxed, pick up your Bible and read your chosen passage through slowly. Don't rush – remember this is God's word for you. If it helps you to concentrate you can read out loud. When you get to the end, stop for a few moments and think about what you've read. When you're ready, read the passage again, pausing again at the end. Repeat for a third time.

By now you may have found that certain words or phrases have stood out for you. What are they? Why have they caught your attention? What do you think God might be saying to you?

Spend a short while reflecting on what you've read and thank God for speaking to you.

The action to follow all of that is fairly obvious really: *read the Bible.*

It's worth the effort, and as we've said, if you want to grow in your faith then it's a vital activity. There are lots of ways to get more out of the Bible.

- You can get study notes that will open up a few verses of the Bible and help you understand what's going on. 'Word 4 U 2Day' is free and available online, as a podcast, as an email or in print. It's a good place to start if you just want a verse a day with a bit of a reflection (visit http://www.ucb.co.uk/w4u). If you want something a bit meatier, have a look at the bookstall in your church – there are bound to be some recommendations.
- Reading the Bible in a year, as we've already noted, is a great way to get into the word of God. Soul Survivor, an organization that runs an annual festival for young people, has published a version of the Bible divided up into daily chunks. You can buy a copy of its *Bible in One Year* from a bookseller and then follow study notes online at http://thebibleinoneyear.wordpress.com/.
- You can get hold of a study Bible, which will have introductions to books and details on what some of the verses mean. I love the *Renovare Spiritual Formation Bible*, which includes a lot of detailed notes. *The Youth Bible* published by Nelson/Word is also good, and there are dozens of other options available. Why not find a Christian bookshop near you and just go and dig through their Bible section until you find one you like the look of, or shop online if that's not an option.

THE APOSTLES' TEACHING

- Lots of churches now podcast their Sunday sermons, so you can have a search on iTunes or any podcast provider and see if there are any that you like. You could ask your vicar or your youth leader which they would recommend.
- Some organizations have recorded the whole Bible, so you can listen to a bit of it every day – see http://godsipod.com/.

Sometimes living in a world that's so full of information might feel overwhelming, but it also means that getting our hands on God's word has never been easier. The Bible is reproduced in loads of different styles to suit every taste – it's just a case of trying some or all of the options and finding a way that suits you. Dig in!

CHAPTER 2

FELLOWSHIP

DO YOU REMEMBER WHEN...
...YOU SAID YOU WOULD
CONTINUE IN FELLOWSHIP?

BISHOP PAUL:

At confirmations I love seeing family and friends gathered together to share in the service with those being confirmed. It's a picture of being in the business of following Jesus together. While each of us has to make our own decision to follow Jesus, and day by day has to decide to continue to do so, we're not alone.

I'm privileged to have met Christians from all over the world. I've learnt a lot from friends in countries like Russia, Rwanda, Argentina and Iran, as well as in the UK. I need the insights they bring about God, his word and his ways. I need their encouragement and help. They also need mine. We need fellowship, not a nice 'holy huddle' gathering together away from the rest of the world. We need to help each other live for Jesus out in the world – in school, college, work, home, sports club, dance studio, parties. We help each other grow as Christians.

What's helped me most over the years has been friends with whom I can be completely honest and who help me when I make mistakes. I'm glad there are those who hold me to account for living a life worthy of Jesus Christ and I'm honoured that others ask me to do the same for them. We can't follow Jesus alone – God has given us one another to work together and build each other up in the faith. Studying the Bible, worshipping, praying and helping one another is vital. Do not neglect to meet with other Christians in fellowship together.

One of the things that I love to do in my spare time is to go running. Until I turned 30 I simply hated all exercise, and then for some reason I suddenly decided that I needed to get fit. I'd tried going to gyms and the like before but never really enjoyed them. I figured that if I took up running I could get fit – it was cheap and I could step out of the door and begin my exercise straight away.

For quite a long time I ran by myself, but before long it just got a bit boring. I was running some good distances but it meant that I was out by myself for an hour or more, and the running started to lose its appeal. I decided that

> **EVERY DAY THEY CONTINUED TO MEET TOGETHER IN THE TEMPLE COURTS. THEY BROKE BREAD IN THEIR HOMES AND ATE TOGETHER WITH GLAD AND SINCERE HEARTS, PRAISING GOD AND ENJOYING THE FAVOUR OF ALL THE PEOPLE. (ACTS 2:46-47 NIV)**

if I wanted to get better and enjoy running a bit more I'd need to run with other people, so I joined a running club. It's made an amazing difference. Going out with other people means that I can run further and faster, and at the same time I can learn good training regimes and what I should do if I get injured along the way. I've made some new friends, some of whom I'd now class as good friends. I've taken part in races and generally become a much better athlete.

One of the things that people noticed about the early Christians was that they spent a lot of time together. Acts 2 paints a picture of a community of people who ate together, shared their possessions and spent lots of time together. They met together daily, both in their homes and out in the public square. These people loved to be together and they loved to take their message out into the open air.

Does that sound good to you? Do you like the idea of being part of a group that spends so much time with each other? Do you like the picture of people who are willing to sell their possessions in order that others who have less don't go without?

To me it sounds amazing, challenging, but a wonderful way to live your life!

That picture of church might not sound much like what we're used to in many places these days. For lots of us, 'church' is simply the thing we do on a Sunday morning; we might even think it just means the building that a bunch of Christians gather in. The thought of a group of people sitting together regularly in each others' homes, eating together and sharing their possessions, might seem very strange!

If it's all right, I'd like to share a bit of Greek with you. Trust me on this – it's not as scary as it might sound . . .

The original Bible texts were written in ancient languages that are no longer used every day. Hebrew, Greek and Latin, the three languages that our Bibles are translated from, are all very 'rich' languages. For instance, in English we have one word for love – it's 'love'. I use the same word to describe the love I have for my wife, my children, my cat, going running and eating chocolate. In Greek there are four words that all mean different kinds of love (they're *agape*, *eros*, *philia* and *storge* if you're interested – Google them if you want definitions!).

In English the word 'church' usually brings to mind a big pointy building where Christian people gather on a Sunday morning. But the Greek word that Bible scholars most regularly translate as church is *ecclesia*.

In Acts 19 there's a story about Paul visiting the Greek city of Ephesus. Ephesus was the home city of the temple of the goddess Artemis. The temple was huge and it attracted thousands of visitors. At its centre was a huge statue of Artemis. As a memento of their trip, visitors would buy a silver replica of the statue, just as you might buy a miniature Eiffel Tower if you visited Paris today.

When Paul arrived at the city he started to tell people about Jesus. One of the things he told them was that being a follower of Jesus meant that they didn't need to buy trinkets – Jesus was alive and therefore little silver statues were no good to Christians. Now put yourself in the place of the people who were making these souvenirs. If your livelihood is based on the sale of small silver statues and someone starts telling people that they don't need to buy them any more, you're going to be pretty hacked off.

One of these silversmiths was a guy named Demetrius, and he was so angry with Paul that he got a group of like-minded people together to demand that the city council throw Paul out of Ephesus for good. In fact there was something of a riot.

Do you want to guess what the Greek word is for this small group of likeminded silversmiths? It's *ecclesia*. This word that we translate as 'big stone building where Christians gather' can also be used to describe a small group of angry silversmiths who started a riot.

FELLOWSHIP

Today there's no doubt that when we use the word 'church' we're talking about a Christian congregation and more specifically the building where they meet. There are still all kinds of different churches but they all share this common name. When we read the word 'church' in the Bible we need to realize that it's referring to something different from what we might be used to now. In the biblical sense the word is used to describe any group of people who gather together with something in common, so the groups of Christians who got together in each others' houses or in the temple courts were 'churches' in the real sense. It also means that when you get together with other Christians with the purpose of growing together in your faith, you're doing 'church' in this biblical sense of the word.

I often hear people telling me that they're Christians but that they don't go to church. Lots of people are convinced that they can carry on in the Christian faith without having to be members of a greater community, and while that might be true, it seems like a pretty poor way to try to keep going as a Christian. Just like me and my running, I know that I need to be part of a group of runners if I want to get better at running. If I want to grow as a Christian then I need to spend time with other Christians.

For the majority of us, a traditional view of church is still the best way for us to get the fellowship we promised we'd continue in at our confirmation. Although I've never met anyone who loves every part of a normal Sunday-morning meeting, there's definitely something very special about being with people of different ages and backgrounds. Some of us love the music; others can't stand it. Some find the prayers too long and wordy; others find them deeply moving. I've preached sermons that some people found truly inspiring and others mindnumbingly dull. It's just like any family: there are things that we'll enjoy about being together and things we'll struggle with.

The key to surviving in church is to find other groups and communities that you can be part of *in addition* to your regular church attendance. I'll suggest some things you can try in the 'React' section below.

It really is virtually impossible to survive and grow on your own as a Christian. We need other Christians around us who we can pray with, talk about things with and read the Bible with.

REACT

If normal Sunday services were the only way I spent time with other Christians then I'd never have grown in my faith. My church is quite traditional – we sit in lines, we sing songs together, we listen politely when someone at the front does a talk or reads prayers, and at a push we have a cup of coffee and a biscuit when the service finishes. While there's nothing wrong with that, I also need to be able to chat, argue and eat food with people. Relationships are built much better in that kind of environment than in a traditional church service. Here are some of the ways that I get that kind of thing. You may want to try some of these ideas yourself.

SMALL GROUPS

I've been a member of all sorts of small groups over the years. Most of them have involved food! At the church where I'm a youth worker we hold a small group on a Sunday morning. We start off along with the adults in church for the first couple of songs and the Bible reading, and then we escape to one of the church rooms. We usually start by having breakfast together and then we talk about a 'big question' of some kind (this Sunday we were trying to work out why God doesn't always answer our prayers . . .). We always start by lighting a candle to remind ourselves that Jesus (the Light of the World) is in the room with us, and then we tuck into croissants and toast. We light the candle before breakfast because we believe that the time we spend eating together is just as much 'church' as the time we spend reading the Bible or praying.

In the past I've also been a part of a small group for people 'like me', that is, young men from the church who wanted to spend an evening together. We'd get together once a month, usually around a meal (no surprise there), and we'd chat, sometimes about a book we were all reading, sometimes just about what we'd been up to since we last met.

I know groups of young people that have got together to play guitars or to help out in a local old people's home. What you get together to do really doesn't matter, as long as you're getting together for the purposes of getting to know Jesus better and to grow in your faith.

If you're not a member of some kind of small group then why not try to set one up? It might be as simple as a group of friends getting together during the lunch break at school (in some cases this might be called a Christian Union), or you might want to invite people back to your house after school – I run a small group for boys in years 7 and 8 that meets in one of their living rooms. If you haven't got the confidence to start something by yourself, have a chat with a friend who's also a Christian, or maybe your youth leader or vicar, and see what ideas you can come up with.

'FRESH EXPRESSIONS' OF CHURCH

In recent years the Church of England and the Methodist Church have encouraged people to think of as many different kinds of church as they can – they call them Fresh Expressions. I've seen and heard of some amazing examples. One group meets every Sunday in a pub in the town near the traditional church. They knew that some people were uncomfortable with going to a normal church building so they took their meetings into a place where they thought they could relax. Another group I know of feel closest to God when they're skating, so their youth worker organized a kind of Church outdoors at a skate park – they call it the Church of Flow. And a group near Bournemouth bought a beach hut where they could go with their friends to surf and then have a place to sit and chat, read the Bible and pray.

Starting a different form of church might seem really daunting, but if you just think of it as a group of people getting together because they share a common interest with the intention of getting to know Christ better, then it seems a little less frightening!

REFLECT

The Bible has some vivid pictures for the Church. Use these reflections to help you think about how amazing it is to be part of that community.

THE BODY

In 1 Corinthians the Church is described as a body – read 1 Corinthians 12.12–26. Do you see that you're an important part of the body, no matter who you are or what you can offer? Which part of the body do you think you are? Why? Are you playing your part fully? Is there anybody in your church that you think is undervalued? Can you think of a way to help them? Maybe you could write them a letter thanking them for what they do, or give them a small gift, a card with a Bible verse on it maybe. Could you make a commitment to pray for your church leaders? Or your youth leaders? Is there anyone who you used to see at church regularly but hasn't been around? Perhaps you could get in touch with them and let them know that you've missed them!

THE BRIDE

In Revelation the Church is described as a bride. Sometimes we can be really grumpy about our churches; we complain that they don't do what we want them to do; we say they're boring or irrelevant or that we don't like them much . . . When you go to a wedding there's always that amazing moment when everyone suddenly goes quiet and you know that the bride is coming into the building – everyone turns and looks, and all of you, as one, think the same thing: 'Wow, she's so beautiful.' If the Bible compares the Church to a bride, then perhaps we should try to view it like that too. Do you need to say sorry to God for times when you've complained about your church? How can you get involved in making your church even more beautiful?

CHAPTER 3

BREAKING BREAD

DO YOU REMEMBER WHEN...
...YOU SAID YOU WOULD
CONTINUE IN THE
BREAKING OF BREAD?

BREAKING BREAD

BISHOP PAUL:

Taking part in Holy Communion needs to be a really regular part of your life, if at all possible. Jesus was very clear with his followers that they should break bread and drink from the cup of wine together whenever they met. This was the way that the first Christians remembered everything about Jesus, but especially about his suffering, death and resurrection. It also reminded them to look forward to the day when Jesus will return as King. They understood that in this act they were proclaiming Jesus' story to the world. It's been a vital part of living for Christ ever since.

Holy Communion is an act of celebration and thanksgiving. We thank God for all he's done for us and the whole of creation in and through the dying and rising of Jesus. In Holy Communion we also look to the future, to the day when Jesus will come again and God's kingdom will be seen in its completeness. It's also a fresh act of being sent out into the world to live for Jesus, for we can't keep this exciting good news to ourselves.

I love the way that, kneeling or standing together to receive the bread and wine, there can be people of all ages: rich and poor; healthy and sick; coming from many different nations; doing all kinds of jobs. Yet all recognize that they're equal before God: equally in need of forgiveness; equally in need of God's strength; equally called to be like Jesus in the world. Holy Communion is a way of being renewed by God. As we take the bread and wine, God, in a mysterious way, meets with us. He assures us of his love. He strengthens us to serve him.

OPENER

Is there something about you that people recognize as uniquely you? It might be a phrase that you say regularly, or perhaps you have a dress style distinctive from your friends. There's a girl at my youth group with curly hair, and rather than a lot of people with curls who might wear their hair tied back, or hidden somehow, she wears it as big as she can get it. It's very cool and very distinctive.

Some people really like to be easily recognized, to stand out from the crowd. Three days before the events in the Bible passage on the right, Jesus had been crucified. His friends think he's dead, and despite some stories from some of

> **WHEN HE WAS AT THE TABLE WITH THEM, HE TOOK BREAD, GAVE THANKS, BROKE IT AND BEGAN TO GIVE IT TO THEM. THEN THEIR EYES WERE OPENED AND THEY RECOGNISED HIM, AND HE DISAPPEARED FROM THEIR SIGHT.**
> **(LUKE 24.30-32 NIV)**

them that he's been seen alive again, the two Luke talks of aren't convinced and so are making the long journey back from Jerusalem to their home in Emmaus, presumably to go back to their old lives, the adventure with Jesus finished.

While they're walking a man comes and joins them – we know that it's Jesus but for some reason they don't recognize him – and as they walk he tells them incredible stories about prophets and history. The men listen, totally enthralled, and when they reach their house they invite the stranger in to spend the evening with them.

They get the meal ready and then the man takes the bread, holds it in the air, gives thanks to God for it and then breaks it. In a flash the men realize who they've been walking with. It's Jesus – they recognized him by the way he broke the bread.

Breaking bread together is really important for Christians. It's one of the ways we mark ourselves out. You may have been taking the bread and wine at church for years or it may be that you had to wait until after you were confirmed, but either way, hopefully you're now taking part in this special activity.

Eating with people is really important – there's something special about sharing a meal with others. Somehow when we're eating we talk together more easily, we relax. It's a place where we can laugh together or talk about things that are difficult. I don't know what it is about food, but it changes the way we interact with another person. You might say that it's sacred. I used to be the youth worker for a church near Guildford, and there was one particular coffee shop in the town where you could guarantee that you'd find a youth worker from one of the local churches meeting with a young person to chat over coffee and a cake. As I mentioned in the previous chapter, the church where I work now even has a Sunday-morning congregation that meets in a local pub – for them church takes place over a bacon sandwich and a cuppa.

A friend of mine reckons that pretty much every major story in the Bible happens around food. Whether it's Adam and Eve eating the fruit in Genesis or the feast that will take place in heaven in Revelation, food is really important in the Jewish and Christian traditions.

The meal that we have at church, which we call Holy Communion or the Eucharist, reminds us of a really important night in Jesus' life. The evening before Jesus was crucified coincided with the Jewish festival of Passover – a special day when Jewish families share a meal together to remember the night when the Hebrews were set free from slavery in Egypt. Jesus was sharing the Passover meal with his friends, and while he was eating he did two slightly strange things. First he took the bread that was on the table, held it in the air, thanked God for it and then passed it around. As people were eating he told them that the bread was his body, which had been broken for them. 'Do this', he says, 'in remembrance of me'. Somehow, taking a bite of bread and remembering that Jesus was broken on a cross becomes a really important thing to do for a Christian.

Later in the meal he takes a cup of wine, again he holds it up, thanks God for it and then passes it on to his friends. As they each take a mouthful he tells them that the wine is like his blood and that whenever they drink it, it will remind them that his blood was 'poured out' for them and for everyone, for the forgiveness of sins.

That last meal with his friends was so important that most Christian churches still act it out regularly so that they don't forget about it. In fact if you're part of an Anglican church then you can be pretty sure that most Sundays your church will celebrate the Eucharist.

The eucharistic meal has been a source of all sorts of discussion and debate over the centuries for the Church. Every tradition celebrates it slightly differently, and even in the Anglican Church we have different views on it. All that discussion hints at just how important the Eucharist is to Christians.

The liturgy we use in Anglican churches has been carefully crafted to make sure we're prepared for the moment when we take the bread and the wine. We need to spend time in confession before we eat and drink, sifting through our lives and bringing before God any sin that we have to sort out, asking for his forgiveness and allowing him to make us pure. We also share the peace with other churchgoers before we take Communion. It's a sign that we think Communion is so important that we have to make sure we're at peace with the rest of the congregation before we take it.

All this might make you wonder why it's so important to remember Jesus' death like this. It might seem a bit morbid to spend so much time and effort remembering something so tragic. The fact is that Christ's death on the cross is absolutely central to the Christian faith. It's the point in history when everything changed. You could say that everything that happened before Christ's death on the cross was building up to that moment and that it's shaped the whole of history from that point onwards. And of course the most amazing thing about Christ's death was that it didn't mark the end. The people who crucified him might have been celebrating that he was gone, but that's because they didn't know the end of the story. Three days after his death, Christ came back to life. The Eucharist doesn't just remind us of Christ's death – it's far more than that, for it also reminds us that in Jesus there is new life.

The Eucharist changes us, and it reminds us of the change that happened when we became Christians. It reminds us that the old life has died and that we're made new – children of God, forgiven and set free! We take the Eucharist so seriously because it changes us – we leave the Communion table different from when we arrived. We've remembered Christ's death, and it affects everything that we do from that time on. We view the world differently because of that moment.

The fact that the Communion service centres around the simple act of eating bread and drinking wine makes us aware of the fact that with God even the most ordinary things become super-important. A Jewish family would have had bread and wine at every dinner, and it's these everyday things that Jesus turns into the most important symbols of our faith for every Christian since that supper some 2,000 years ago.

For me it also shows that God makes all things special. There's a well-known writer called Rob Bell who teaches that, with God, 'everything is spiritual'. By making the bread and wine special or 'sacramental', Jesus is saying that, with God, these ordinary things become special. It also helps us see that all the things we do – in our work, our study, our interactions with other people – become sacred moments when done with God – moments where God can do amazing things and in which we can worship him.

It means that you don't have to wait until you're involved in a church activity to meet with God. It's why some people pray before each meal or others before they go to sleep or as soon as they wake up: they want to remind themselves that each and every thing they do is spiritual. If taking Communion is a big sacrament then you could think of eating, sleeping and even breathing as mini-sacraments. (Some Hebrew people even had special prayers that they said before they went to the toilet – for them *everything* was spiritual!)

REFLECT

The liturgy for Holy Communion produced by the Church of England talks about how important it is to prepare yourself properly for the service. In fact the first half of the Communion service is called the Preparation. If we're to take the Eucharist seriously then we need to make sure we're properly ready for it.

You might want to try the following prayers as a way to get yourself fit for Holy Communion.

COME, HOLY GHOST

We start by asking the Holy Spirit to come and fill us, to help us to become aware of God's presence with us and to help us search ourselves to see what we need to change before we take Communion (don't worry too much about the old language or some unfamiliar words – just use it as a prayer for God to pour out his love on us).

Come, Holy Ghost, our souls inspire,
And lighten with celestial fire;
Thou the anointing Spirit art,
Who dost thy sevenfold gifts impart.

Thy blessed unction[2] from above
Is comfort, life and fire of love;
Enable with perpetual light
The dullness of our blinded sight.

Anoint and cheer our soiled face
With the abundance of thy grace;
Keep far our foes, give peace at home;
Where thou art guide no ill can come.

Teach us to know the Father, Son,
And thee, of Both, to be but One;
That through the ages all along
This may be our endless song:

Praise to thy eternal merit,
Father, Son and Holy Spirit.
Amen.[3]

EXHORTATION

The Bible has very strong warnings about how we prepare ourselves for taking Holy Communion (read 1 Corinthians 11.27–29 for St Paul's warnings to the Christians who lived in the city of Corinth). Take this moment to sit quietly and think through what you're going to do at the Communion Table – are you prepared?

SUMMARY OF THE LAW

The Bible contains all we need to know about what God expects of us, so at this point you could remind yourself about what it says – either read the ten commandments as written in Exodus 20.1–17 or use the words below, which are Jesus' summary of the Law.

Our Lord Jesus Christ said:
The first commandment is this:
'Hear, O Israel, the Lord our God is the only Lord.
You shall love the Lord your God with all your heart,
with all your soul, with all your mind,
and with all your strength.'

The second is this: 'Love your neighbour as yourself.'
There is no other commandment greater than these.
On these two commandments hang all the law and the prophets.

Amen. Lord, have mercy.[4]

SILENCE FOR REFLECTION

Think over the words you've just said. Is there anywhere that you're falling short? Are there commandments you're neglecting or are there times and places where you've failed to love God or your neighbour?

CONFESSION

Use this prayer or a similar one to say sorry to God for your shortcomings.

Lord God,
I have sinned against you;
I have done evil in your sight.
I am sorry and repent.
Have mercy on me according to your love.
Wash away my wrongdoing and cleanse me from my sin.
Renew a right spirit within me
and restore me to the joy of your salvation;
through Jesus Christ my Lord.
Amen.[5]

ABSOLUTION

When we ask God to forgive us, he always does because of the sacrifice that Jesus made on the cross. Read these words and imagine that God himself speaks them to you.

The God who loved the world so much
that he sent his Son to be your Saviour
forgives you your sins
and makes you holy to serve him in the world,
through Jesus Christ your Lord.
Amen.[6]

REACT

One person who completely changed after eating a meal with Jesus was Zacchaeus. You probably know this very famous story from Luke 19 about a tax-collector who was too short to see Jesus when he came to his town. He climbed a tree to get a better view and was astonished when, rather than passing by, Jesus stopped, looked up into the branches and invited himself round for dinner.

After the meal the change in Zacchaeus was unmistakable. He stepped out of his house and promised to pay back every person that he'd ever cheated, to make his peace with the world properly. He knew that he'd done all sorts of things wrong and that he'd upset and cheated lots of people, so he set out to make his peace with as many as he could. It was an amazingly courageous thing to do, and he's famous because of it to this day.

BREAKING BREAD

I wonder if there's anyone you need to make your peace with? Is there anyone you've wronged? Maybe there's someone you've gossiped about or someone you always argue with. Can you think if there's anyone who might harbour bad feelings about you because of something you've done to them? If so, then I wonder whether you might want to follow Zacchaeus' example and try to make your peace – to go and find that person, tell them you're sorry and offer to make things up with them if you can. This isn't an easy request at all, and there may be people who you can't ever imagine saying sorry to or making peace with. If that's the case then you might want to pray about the situation and get advice from an older Christian before you do anything rash.

CHAPTER 4

THE PRAYERS

DO YOU REMEMBER WHEN... ...YOU SAID YOU WOULD CONTINUE IN THE PRAYERS?

THE PRERS

BISHOP PAUL:

After following Jesus for many years I cannot say that I always find prayer easy. Sometimes it's very hard; sometimes it happens more easily. Prayer is both talking to God, and listening to him.

Often I talk to God in my own words, although sometimes I just can't find the words to say. I'm so glad that God doesn't ask me to get the words right all the time. At other times I use other people's words. It's great that God has given us lots of help with this. The prayers of the Bible and the prayers others have written through the ages often give me the words I need. But in both types there are still times when it feels like my words don't rise through the ceiling.

I listen to God by being quiet and still. As I read the words of the Bible I'm seeking to understand what God is saying through this precious book. I also listen for God through the ideas and the suggestions of others, and through events that take place.

For some of my praying I sit quietly. Sometimes I find it helpful to kneel, at other times I stand. But then there are times when I go for a walk and pray out loud, telling God just how I feel and what I think.

I also find it really helpful to pray with other people, both in formal services and informally, with one or two others or a larger group.

One thing that helps me pray for others is knowing that I need to be prayed for myself. At its heart, prayer is not about asking God for things, rather it's about seeking to line up our lives and thoughts with God's. Prayer expresses our reliance on God to lead, equip and empower us. It's about placing others and our world into God's hands, knowing they're his to care for.

Sometimes I listen to my breathing and remember that I rely on breathing God *in* through prayer and breathing *out* my faults and failures for God to deal with. We need to pray as much as to breathe.

OPENER

I have a best friend. We do loads of things together, we go out for coffee, we take our children to the park, we walk his dog and so on. We talk to each other a lot too, sometimes just over a drink, sometimes at each other's house. We talk on the phone, we text, we Facebook.

Basically we're in communication with each other, often and in lots of different ways.

If someone told me I was only allowed to communicate with my friend in one particular way or in one particular place, I'd find it very odd. That's not how friendships work.

> **PRAY IN THE SPIRIT ON ALL OCCASIONS WITH ALL KINDS OF PRAYERS AND REQUESTS. WITH THIS IN MIND, BE ALERT AND ALWAYS KEEP ON PRAYING FOR ALL THE LORD'S PEOPLE.**
> **(EPHESIANS 6.18 NIV)**

That might be a bit of an obvious analogy, but it doesn't make it any less true. One role that God plays in our lives is as a friend, and as with all friends, that relationship develops when we communicate with each other.

Prayer is essentially communicating with God.

THE PRAYERS

The word 'prayer' means all sorts of different things for different people. For lots of us it will summon up pictures of sitting at infant school – hands together and eyes closed – and repeating the Lord's Prayer together. It might make us think of that thing we do in church when someone at the front reads prayers they've written while we sit quietly and listen (or not). It might summon up a picture of sitting in a youth group in a circle and taking turns to talk to God and each other about the things that concern us and that we want him to get involved with.

Whatever our experience, for most of us prayer is a combination of talking and occasionally listening. So why in Ephesians 6.18 does Paul refer to 'all kinds of prayers and requests'? How many different kinds of talking and listening can there possibly be?

The truth, of course, is that prayer is so much more than just talking and listening. To be honest, such a two-dimensional experience of prayer would only be enjoyed by a very small group of people who are comfortable with that kind of communication. Prayer can be all sorts of things – there can be as much variety as you like.

The place to look in the Bible for a really good rundown on prayer is Psalms. Psalms is a collection of prayers written as poems and songs. You could think of Psalms as the prayer book at the centre of the Bible (it's in the Old Testament). Written by lots of different people over hundreds of years, the individual psalms demonstrate how to pray in every situation and with every conceivable example of human emotion. If you think praying is just quietly asking God for help with things, think again: there's some really angry stuff in Psalms. For instance:

Wake up! Do something, Lord!
Why are you sleeping?
Don't desert us for ever.
Why do you keep looking away?
Don't forget our sufferings
and all our troubles.
(Psalm 44.23–24 CEV)

That's quite heavy – the Sons of Korah (who wrote the prayer) have just accused God of sleeping and deserting them. That sounds like thunderbolt-time to me!

Possibly the most passionate prayer ever was the one Jesus prayed on the cross: 'My God, my God, why have you forsaken me?' As he dies, Jesus feels as though God has left him all alone, and so he cries out these words, which are a quote from another psalm.

So the first thing to learn about prayer is that it doesn't just mean sitting in a circle quietly asking God for things. Prayer is a conversation with God about the stuff that really matters to us – it's us sharing with God what's on our heart and then asking his help or his response.

Another issue might be that we don't know where to pray. Lots of us will be used to praying in school or church, but it might not have occurred to us that we can pray elsewhere. Again, some of us might be used to praying in a group, but praying on our own might feel a bit daunting. We might have images of kneeling beside our bed praying before we go to sleep or maybe saying a quick grace before a meal, but perhaps to us prayer doesn't extend much beyond that.

THE PRAYERS

Prayer isn't really restricted to a particular place or time, and in fact for many Christians, prayer feels like a constant conversation with God. I once heard someone say that real prayer was 'having a heart that is turned towards God', and I think I totally get that. It's about being the kind of person who always has God on their mind and is in constant communication with him, just as I am with my best friend.

That doesn't mean, of course, that special prayer times aren't also of real importance. Lots of Christians have 'quiet times', special times each day when they stop and deliberately spend some time talking to God. Lots of people in the Bible had prayer times. Jesus himself 'often withdrew to lonely places and prayed' (Luke 5.16 NIV).

If that's not a habit you're used to, then it's one well worth trying to get into, and much of the React section (on page 49) will be tied up with suggestions for things you can do to help you with that personal prayer.

For me, one of the hardest things about praying is knowing where to start. In the Ephesians passage we started with, Paul tells us to pray for all people. I know a couple of hundred people or more, plus the many more acquaintances I might have, not to mention the millions that I'll never meet. It can be easy to try to start praying and quickly give up, overwhelmed by the whole thing. It can be useful to have some kind of formula for prayer, to divide it up into chunks and make it a bit easier to approach.

A formula I find really helpful is to use *adoration*, *confession*, *thanksgiving* and *supplication* prayers – or ACTS.

Adoration is about telling God all the marvellous things that we think about him. Do you ever go to the beach or stand on a hill or maybe even stand at the foot of a huge skyscraper and find yourself feeling totally awed by how amazing it is? That's what it's like to sit and think about God. When I come into prayer I'm getting ready to talk to the Creator of the universe, the One who threw billions of stars into space, who crafted enormous white-hot suns and the tiniest of bacteria. It can be quite overwhelming. Adoration is a great place to start prayer because it reminds us who we're talking to. If you're stuck for words, why not look at some of the famous prayers of adoration in Psalms – a great place to start is Psalm 145:

The LORD is gracious and compassionate,
slow to anger and rich in love.

The LORD is good to all;
he has compassion on all he has made.
All your works praise you, LORD;
your faithful people extol you.
They tell of the glory of your kingdom
and speak of your might,
so that all people may know of your mighty acts
and the glorious splendour of your kingdom.
Your kingdom is an everlasting kingdom,
and your dominion endures through all generations.

The LORD is trustworthy in all he promises
and faithful in all he does.

(Psalm 145.8–13 NIV)

THE PRAYERS

The trouble with recognizing how great God is is that it can leave you feeling pretty lowly. You think about how wonderful the God of the universe is and you're reminded of all the things in you that are wrong. So it's fairly natural to follow adoration with *confession*. Confession is recognizing the things that are wrong in your life and with your attitudes, and asking God to forgive you for those things. If you're looking for some good words to use in your prayers of confession, have a look at Psalm 51 – it's one of the most famous 'sorry' prayers ever written. Alternatively, there are several prayers of confession that you can use from *Common Worship* – for a good selection, see http://www.churchofengland.org/prayer-worship/worship/texts/psalter,-collects-and-other-resources/confessions.aspx.

The incredible thing about God is that when we ask for forgiveness, he always gives it. God really, really loves you, and no matter what you've done wrong he'll always take you back. Being forgiven leaves me feeling really thankful, so after confession I want to give thanks to God (that's what *thanksgiving* means), both for forgiving me and for all the other good stuff he's done in my life. It's only natural.

Finally, when I've finished thanking God I feel ready to ask him for his help, to tell him what's on my heart and to ask him to respond. A word for that kind of prayer is *supplication*, which literally means coming to someone and asking them for things.

And there you have it – a really simple way to structure your prayer time. You see, sometimes there just seems to be so much to pray for that we simply don't know where to start. Or sometimes we get so bogged down in asking for stuff that we never do anything else except ask. ACTS is a really easy way to pray – adoration, confession, thanksgiving and supplication.

Whatever way you choose to pray (and there are plenty of examples in the next React and Reflect sections), the most important thing is actually to pray. Building a relationship with someone depends on conversation, and it's no different with God. He wants you to get to know him as well as possible, and that means talking to him and, more importantly, allowing space to listen or just be still.

Even using ACTS, praying can be difficult if you're the kind of person who gets easily distracted or whose mind wanders. If that's the case, here are some ideas to help you concentrate.

PRAYING AT THE POINT OF A PEN

OK, so it sounds a bit grand, but it simply means writing out your prayers. I used to keep a book that each day I'd get out and divide into four sections. I'd write an 'A' in one section, 'C' in another, then 'T' and 'S' in a third and fourth. Then rather than closing my eyes and trying to talk to God in my head, I'd write the prayers out instead. It meant that I kept my focus and also that later on I could go back and remind myself what I'd been praying about at a certain time. You could even start a blog and keep your prayers going that way.

OBJECTS

Sometimes you can help your concentration by simply having something to look at or hold. That might mean having a picture or, if it's safe, a candle. You might even want to try to get hold of a cross that you can look at or hold if it helps you concentrate. I have two photos of lighthouses in stormy seas, and looking at them really helps me concentrate – they remind me that God is strong even when everything else seems uncertain, just like the lighthouses.

THE JESUS PRAYER

Often you might find that you don't actually want to pray about anything specific, either because you can't think of anything or you just don't feel in that kind of mood. The Jesus Prayer is a prayer that people have been saying for centuries. The words are very simple: 'Lord Jesus Christ, Son of God, have mercy on me, a sinner.'

Traditionally people say the words slowly and quietly over and over again until they just flow very naturally. You can say them in time with your breathing so that you breathe in as you say, 'Lord Jesus Christ, Son of God,' and out as you say, 'have mercy on me, a sinner'. In the past people have used a string with knots in it or a string of beads (sometimes called a rosary) in order to keep count of how many times they've prayed the prayer, so you can repeat it tens, hundreds or even thousands of times. I know it sounds a bit odd, but try it and see what happens. If you find it strange or unhelpful, leave it there, but you might discover that the words speak to you about Jesus.

PRAYING WITH OTHERS

If you find praying on your own really hard it's worth persevering, but it's also good to pray with others. Lots of Christians meet up in threes, or prayer triplets, with people they know really well and trust. That way you regularly spend time in prayer and also have the support and help of others. And it means that you can chat over what you've prayed about in the past and how God has answered your prayers.

ONLINE PRAYER COMMUNITY

There are now also several places where you can go to join in with daily prayer online. The Church of England publishes its daily offices at http://www.churchofengland.org/prayer-worship/join-us-in-daily-prayer.aspx. You can choose between contemporary or traditional language and have a choice of morning, evening or night prayer.

The Jesuits (a religious order following the teachings of the Catholic Church) also run online prayer communities at http://www.jesuit.org.uk/spirituality/prayer.htm. You can choose between 'Sacred Space', a ten-minute order of daily prayer, or 'Pray-as-you-go', a downloadable audio prayer time.

REFLECT

For this chapter, this section is going to be very simple. You might remember that we said prayer is more than just talking, that it's also about listening. We live in a world that gives us very little time to be quiet and still, so we're going to give that a try now. All I want you to do is get yourself into a quiet place where you're comfortable, and then sit in absolute silence. If that idea freaks you out, start with a very short time – even 30 seconds of quiet can feel like a really good use of time. Try asking God to speak to you while you sit quietly – the words can be really simple: 'God, please would you speak to me while I sit here in silence. Thank you.'

If you manage 30 seconds this time, why not try a minute next time or even longer? I work with someone who each year goes away and spends a whole week in silence . . .

THE PRAYERS

If you find it really hard to focus or relax, you might want to try a centring exercise like this one by Mark Yaconelli:

> Imagine that you are walking down a staircase that begins in your mind and winds, slowly down to your heart. Take a few moments to imagine walking this staircase, leaving all the many worries and thoughts behind, slowly descending into a secret room or chapel within your heart where God waits to pray with you.[7]

Or try this breathing exercise from the same book:

> Close your eyes and simply notice your breathing. Take a moment to imagine the air in the room is filled with God's light and God's love. For the next few minutes just pay attention to your breathing, imagining with each in-breath that you are breathing in God's love, and with every out-breath that you are releasing every distraction, every anxiety, every tension and resistance to God.[8]

CHAPTER 5

RESISTING EVIL

DO YOU REMEMBER WHEN...
...YOU SAID YOU WOULD
PERSEVERE IN
RESISTING EVIL?

BISHOP PAUL:

Evil things happen in the world. Just watching the news on TV or opening up a newspaper tells us that very quickly. The danger is that sometimes we therefore see 'evil' as somewhere else other than immediately around us. The truth is that every day, in some way or another, I have to resist evil. I can be tempted to lie, not necessarily outright fibs but exaggeration, or claim more credit for myself than is right. I can be tempted to think more highly of myself than I should. I can think badly of other people. I can say unkind words that hurt other people. So I have to resist evil that comes from within myself. Then images I see on TV or advertising boards can make me reduce women to sexual objects rather than wonderful human beings. I can be caught up in a clamour for revenge or a world of violence rather than being a peacemaker. I have to resist the evil that comes from the world around me, often through the media but also through the words, attitudes and actions of the people I meet in my daily life.

Then there's the reality that the Bible teaches us that there is an evil one, the devil, who'll always tempt me to go away from following Jesus Christ. He'll tempt me to choose an easy life rather than walking 'the way of the cross'.

So resisting evil is a daily reality. It comes at me from outside myself and from within. I can never give up the fight. I have to persist. Fortunately this is part of the work of the Holy Spirit within us all. He gives us strength to persevere, strength to choose to do right rather than give in to evil. Jesus faced temptation throughout his life, not just when he was in the wilderness. He persevered in resisting evil to the very end, and it was very costly for him. I find persevering in resisting evil is tough. Evil is often attractive and easy while doing good can be tough and costly – but it's the way God calls us to go.

OPENER

In a huge number of movies that come out of Hollywood there's a real emphasis on the existence of evil. Harry Potter fights Voldemort and the dark arts, Neo battles Agent Smith in *The Matrix*, Frodo Baggins is pitted against Sauron and the armies of Mordor in *The Lord of the Rings* – even in Disney cartoons there's usually some kind of battle between light and dark, good and evil.

> **PUT ON THE FULL ARMOUR OF GOD, SO THAT YOU CAN TAKE YOUR STAND AGAINST THE DEVIL'S SCHEMES. FOR OUR STRUGGLE IS NOT AGAINST FLESH AND BLOOD, BUT AGAINST THE RULERS, AGAINST THE AUTHORITIES, AGAINST THE POWERS OF THIS DARK WORLD AND AGAINST THE SPIRITUAL FORCES OF EVIL IN THE HEAVENLY REALMS.**
> **(EPHESIANS 6.11-12 NIV)**

And yet in real life we're far more wary of admitting that there might be a dark side, any force other than God and all his goodness.

In the Bible there's absolutely no doubt that this other side exists. And while the language used to describe the enemy can sometimes be a bit confusing, his existence is never in question. Right from the opening pages of the Bible, when the serpent persuades Eve to eat from the tree of the knowledge of good and evil, to its closing pages with the imagery of the enemy being cast into a burning pit, we're reminded time and time again that there's a force out there that wants to bring God's people down. So the first thing to be aware of is that there is an enemy. The devil is real, and he's looking for ways to undermine your faith in God – 1 Peter 5.8 says the devil 'prowls around like a roaring lion looking for someone to devour' (NIV). If you're not already hiding behind the sofa, now might be the time . . .

Before you start to panic, there are some really important things to be aware of. First, the devil submits to God: God is definitely in charge here, and the enemy has to submit to his authority. Second, we can stand against him, and God gives us all that we need in order to do that. Last (spoiler alert), God will win and the enemy will be defeated, of that we have no doubt.

THE DEVIL SUBMITS TO GOD

There was once an incredible man of God. The Bible says that he was 'blameless and upright; he feared God and shunned evil'. The man's name was Job. It goes on to say that one day Satan came to present himself to God. God talks to Satan and draws his attention to Job. He tells him how good he is, boasting about this amazing man who serves him so well. Satan isn't impressed at all; he's convinced that Job only serves God because his life is so easy. He points out how wealthy he is and how good his life is – 'stretch out your hand and strike everything he has,' continues Satan, 'and he will surely curse you to your face'.

It's an odd exchange, and we might expect God to refuse any harm to come to this good man, but instead God, so confident of Job's commitment to him, allows Satan free rein over his life: 'Very well, then, everything he has is in your power,' says God, 'but on the man himself do not lay a finger' (Job 1.1, 11, 12 NIV).

Did you notice the power that God retains in this encounter? It may look sometimes like our world is totally out of control, but we know Satan can't do anything that God hasn't allowed him to. Sometimes Satan is described as the 'prince' of this world, but that God is very much still the King. In the story of Job, Satan wreaks havoc on his life, but he has to stick within the boundaries God has laid down – he can't simply do as he pleases.

WE CAN STAND AGAINST THE DEVIL

This second point, then, is also key: God has given us everything we need to be able to resist anything that the devil can throw at us. With God on our side we're stronger than the devil. Paul writes that God 'will not let you be tempted beyond what you can bear. But when you are tempted, he will also provide a way out so that you can endure it' (1 Corinthians 10.13 NIV). Paul is keen to tell us that we will be tempted, but that we won't be tempted beyond our ability to resist.

Now for anyone who's stood and looked at that last chocolate in the packet (substitute your particular vice here), this may seem like pretty weak advice. We've all been tempted and we've all failed. That's why in Ephesians 6.10–17, Paul gives us a very clear visual explanation of how we can overcome the enemy. First, though, a little background.

People who lived in Israel at the time of the early Church would have been used to seeing Roman soldiers around. The country was under occupation by a military superpower, and its soldiers maintained a visible presence. So when Paul tells the Ephesians that they need to put on the armour of God, they'd instantly have something to picture.

RESISTING EVIL

Maybe the most surprising thing about Paul's armour is that it isn't particularly supernatural. Everyone knows that if you want to battle vampires you need garlic and a cross, and if you're going after werewolves you need silver bullets. But in order to fight the devil it appears that above all else what you need is common sense.

Paul tells us that, like the Roman soldier, we should start by wearing truth like a belt. Tell the truth, says Paul – don't get caught up in lies and deceit but rather live transparently. Next he tells us to fit the breastplate of righteousness in place. Living righteously means being the kind of person who does the right thing in God's eyes, so you might describe a righteous person as a moral person or simply a good person. He continues through the soldier's arms and armour, advising us to be ready for action – we never know when we might be faced with temptation, so we always need to be on our guard. We need to have faith, to be assured that God is with us and that he can and will protect us; we should wear salvation like a helmet, knowing without any doubt that we're saved; and we're to carry the word of God like a sword, to know what the Bible says and to be ready to call to mind Scriptures that are relevant for any situation.

Like I say, there's no magic in any of that advice but rather the simple instruction to live a Christian faith that's as close to what God asks of us as we can manage. Wearing the armour of God, Paul assures us, will leave us able to stand firm in the face of any of the devil's attacks.

ULTIMATELY THE DEVIL WILL LOSE

This is the ultimate hope for a Christian: it's that we can be absolutely assured that the devil cannot win against God. In fact we believe that when Christ died on the cross, the devil was defeated once and for all. It's a promise that God made right at the start of the Bible. After Adam and Eve have eaten fruit from the tree, God turns to the serpent and assures him that one day one of Eve's children will crush his head. For Christians, this is a clear picture that Christ will defeat the devil. Then in John's prophecy in Revelation, the devil is destroyed once and for all.

No matter how tough things feel day to day, we know that in the end we follow a God who will be victorious. We can trust that the earth will be remade and will be perfect once again, and that all the corruption the devil has brought into the world – sickness, decay and even death – will one day be gone for good.

And I heard a loud voice from the throne saying, 'Look! God's dwelling-place is now among the people, and he will dwell with them. They will be his people, and God himself will be with them and be their God. "He will wipe every tear from their eyes. There will be no more death" or mourning or crying or pain, for the old order of things has passed away.'
(Revelation 21.3–4 NIV)

REACT

St Patrick lived in Ireland in the fourth century. He was the son of a wealthy Roman family who, after being captured and sold into slavery, dedicated his life totally to serving God. He's attributed with bringing the Christian faith to Ireland. Patrick knew he wasn't just fighting a 'flesh and blood' battle against human enemies but also a spiritual battle against the devil.

He composed a prayer that's become known as 'St Patrick's Breastplate'. People still find its words moving and reassuring today, some 1,700 years after they were written.

Often when we pray a prayer we sit in silence or put quiet music on to help us be calm and to relax, but as this prayer is about preparing yourself for battle, you might want to choose something a little more stirring. Use an online music player such as Spotify and search for some battle music from a film – 'The Ride of the Rohirrim' from *The Lord of the Rings*, 'The Battle' from *Gladiator* or 'War' from *Avatar* are all possibilities (you can probably think of far better ones of your own).

Stick the music on, stand up, remember that you're entering a battle and read Patrick's prayer – use the words and the music to help you prepare yourself, strapping on God's armour to help you in the battle.

I bind to myself today
The strong virtue of the Invocation of the Trinity:
I believe the Trinity in the Unity
The Creator of the Universe.

I bind to myself today
The virtue of the Incarnation of Christ with His Baptism,
The virtue of His crucifixion with His burial,
The virtue of His Resurrection with His Ascension,
The virtue of His coming on the Judgement Day.

I bind to myself today
The power of Heaven,
The light of the sun,
The brightness of the moon,
The splendour of fire,
The flashing of lightning,
The swiftness of wind,
The depth of sea,
The stability of earth,
The compactness of rocks.

I bind to myself today
God's Power to guide me,
God's Might to uphold me,
God's Wisdom to teach me,
God's Eye to watch over me,
God's Ear to hear me,
God's Word to give me speech,
God's Hand to guide me,

RESISTING EVIL

God's Way to lie before me,
God's Shield to shelter me,
God's Host to secure me,
Against the snares of demons,
Against the seductions of vices,
Against the lusts of nature,
Against everyone who meditates injury to me,
Whether far or near,
Whether few or with many.

Christ with me, Christ before me,
Christ behind me, Christ within me,
Christ beneath me, Christ above me,
Christ at my right, Christ at my left . . .
Christ in the heart of everyone who thinks of me,
Christ in the mouth of everyone who speaks to me,
Christ in every eye that sees me,
Christ in every ear that hears me.

I bind to myself today
The strong virtue of an invocation of the Trinity,
I believe the Trinity in the Unity
The Creator of the Universe.[9]

REFLECT

Our involvement with the dark side can take all sorts of forms. For some of us it will be very obvious, especially if we're dabbling with anything occult – Ouija boards, tarot cards or other practices obviously not of God. But for most of us it will be in much more subtle ways that we're leaving ourselves open to attack from the enemy – consumerism, pornography or an obsession with our identity and appearance are all subtle ways that the enemy can undermine God's work in our lives.

It's a good practice to look at ourselves to find out what's drawing us away from God so that we can have the knowledge and the strength to do something about it. What follows is an exercise called the Ignatian 'Examen': it's a great way to study yourself to find out where there might be chinks in the armour. It was developed by Ignatius, a Spanish soldier, who was injured in battle in 1521. As he recovered from his injuries he had a conversion experience and found great pleasure reading about Jesus and the Saints (he'd become one of those later himself). He developed a passion for helping people grow in their faith, and wrote down his ideas for how to experience God more in daily life – a book now called the *Spiritual Exercises*.

THE EXAMEN

1. BECOME AWARE OF GOD'S PRESENCE
St Ignatius believed with all his being that God was everywhere and could be found in everything. You didn't have to be in church or any other 'holy' place to have an encounter with God, because God could

be found absolutely everywhere. People find that they can become aware of God's presence in all manner of ways. Sometimes it's good to have something to look at – a picture, a cross or a candle – just an object that reminds you about God and helps you remember that he's with you.

2. REVIEW THE DAY WITH GRATITUDE

The next step is to review the previous day, being thankful to God for all that happened in it. If it's morning, think about what happened yesterday; if it's evening, run your mind over what's happened during today. Can you mentally make a list of all the people you've met, all the things you've seen and done, what you've learnt, what's made you laugh or cry? Thank God for all of them, because God was with you in all of it. I read about someone who sits on her sofa and imagines that God is sitting next to her so that she can chat through her experiences as she would to a friend sitting there with her.

3. PAY ATTENTION TO YOUR EMOTIONS

Ignatius suggests that as you think through your day you should pay particular attention to your emotions. Are there things that make you really happy? Did anything make you feel angry? Is there anything that leaves you feeling guilty or ashamed? It may be that God is trying to tell you something through those emotions, so pay close attention to them. As we think about resisting evil, you may want to pay particular attention to the things that made you angry or ashamed – what do you think God is asking you to do?

4. CHOOSE ONE FEATURE FROM THE DAY AND PRAY ABOUT IT

If something from your day really stands out or causes a particularly strong emotional reaction in you, you might want to make that the main theme of your prayers. Ask God to speak to you about what you thought about, ask him to help you if it's something you're struggling with, or to give you strength if it's something you've got to face up to or confront.

5. LOOK FORWARD TO TOMORROW

Before you close, Ignatius suggests that you should finish by thinking about what you're going to get up to tomorrow and to be excited about the prospect of all that a day might offer. Who will you meet? What will you do? What difference do you think you can make in the world today?

CHAPTER 6

REPENT AND RETURN

DO YOU REMEMBER WHEN...
...YOU SAID THAT, WHENEVER
YOU FALL INTO SIN,
YOU WOULD REPENT AND
RETURN TO THE LORD?

BISHOP PAUL:

I'd love to be perfect, but I'm not. My biggest failing is choosing to do things my own way rather than God's. That's the heart of 'sin'. It's not so much about thinking, doing or saying wrong things or failing to do good things, rather it's about not putting God first (which then leads to thinking, doing or saying wrong and failing to do good). It's failing to resist evil and giving in to it. We all keep doing this – becoming a Christian doesn't make us sin-free. So I need continually to recognize that this is the case, own up to it to God, say sorry and determine with the Holy Spirit's help to live God's way. When Jesus died on the cross he died for all my sins, past, present and future, so I know I'm forgiven. I want to live my life for Jesus now in every way. But I slip up. To repent isn't just to say sorry, it's to change our mind; to turn round again and go God's way – hence 'return to the Lord'.

I'm not alone in this – we all fall short. That's why it's good – and important – to say sorry together in our worship, in what's called the Confession. Here we take time to be still and reflect, then use words to express our sorrow for what we've done wrong personally, and together. Then it's very powerful to hear God's promise of forgiveness (the Absolution) again and again. The amazing thing is, however often I fail, God keeps taking me back. He does the same for you. But this knowledge of forgiveness isn't an excuse to go and do wrong again, rather it inspires us to seek to live God's way. In repenting and returning to the Lord we're committing ourselves afresh to living like Jesus Christ in the power of his Spirit.

OPENER

Once when I spoke to Bishop Paul about confirmation, he told me that when he reaches this part of the service he often adds an extra line. After saying, 'whenever you fall into sin', he adds, 'which you will'.

'Sin' is a funny word – we read it and we start to feel uncomfortable. We know there are things in our lives we get up to that aren't really very good for us, and loads of things we do that are lower than the standards God has for us. Bishop Paul has it right: sin is something

> A THIEF COMES ONLY TO ROB, KILL, AND DESTROY. I CAME SO THAT EVERYONE WOULD HAVE LIFE, AND HAVE IT FULLY.' (JOHN 10.10 CEV)

we all get caught up in, most of us on a daily basis. It should be of some comfort to us that even he, a bishop, still struggles to remain sin-free!

People struggle with all sorts of sins, and the Bible contains lists and lists of things that are less than God expects of us as Christians. Try reading through this list from Galatians:

People's desires make them give in to immoral ways, filthy thoughts, and shameful deeds. They worship idols, practise witchcraft, hate others, and are hard to get along with. People become jealous, angry, and selfish. They not only argue and cause trouble, but they are envious. They get drunk, carry on at wild parties, and do other evil things as well. I told you before, and I am telling you again: no one who does these things will share in the blessings of God's kingdom.

(Galatians 5.19-21 CEV)

REPENT AND RETURN

If you're feeling really brave, you might want to go through the list again and highlight any you struggle with.

I wanted to start with the verse from John 10 because for me it sums up the difference between a life that isn't built on persevering in resisting evil and sin and a life that is.

I know for myself that when I'm stuck in a place where I'm continually turning my back on God and refusing to follow his word and his teaching, it feels like there's a thief in my life. Sin may often feel like it's life-*giving*. There's the initial excitement of breaking the rules and doing our own thing, but in reality it's actually really tiring and exhausting. You see sin is corrosive – it eats away at us and changes us. If you've ever seen metal that's rusted really badly you'll know how weak it is – a piece of steel that once was solid and sound can be crumbled away between your fingers. When sin builds up in our lives it has a similar effect – it's really difficult to stand up and speak confidently about your faith when you're being eaten away by unhealthy behaviour, and rather than a strong faith you end up with something that's weak and fragile and doesn't really stand up to close inspection.

We can get to the stage where we realize that the life we *want* to live, a life that reflects God's glory, is nothing like the life we're *actually* living. You might find that you're pretending to be one person on a Sunday when you're at church with your friends, but midweek you're quite different, or maybe the things that go on in your mind are nothing like the things that come out of your mouth! In Romans, Paul writes that he struggled with exactly this kind of lifestyle clash: 'I don't understand why I act the way I do. I don't do what I know is right. I do the things I hate' (Romans 7.15 CEV).

When we've turned round and are looking at God and walking away from the destructive thing in our lives, *then* we really can know what 'life in all its fullness' is like.

It's difficult to own up to the sins we commit. We don't like to because we think God might be so disappointed with us that he won't love us any more, and we don't want to tell other people because they might think less of us or judge us.

The truth is that God already knows everything about us, all the good and all the bad. When we admit to our sin he won't be shocked because he already knows all about it. And as for his not loving us any more, nothing could be further from the truth. A writer called Philip Yancey describes it like this: 'There is nothing we can do to make God love us more and there is nothing we can do to make God love us less.'[10] When we confess our sins to God and ask for forgiveness, he comes alongside us and he forgives us. It's as though he loves us so much that he can't bear to be cross with us, and he celebrates when we say sorry and do our best to live a different life.

One of the Psalms talks about confession like this: 'How far has the LORD taken our sins from us? Further than the distance from east to west!' (Psalm 103.12 CEV). It's a great image – when we ask for God's forgiveness, he grabs our sin and takes it away from us completely. Some people like to think of it as God completely forgetting what we'd done wrong, as if it had never happened. It's pretty awe-inspiring really!

Telling other people about our sin can be harder than telling God. When my uncle died he left me his old car. It was a great little car, and because he'd only ever used it to drive to the shops and back it hadn't done many miles. I cleaned it up inside and out, I had the engine serviced and I made the inside bright and sparkling. I installed a loud stereo in it and drove it all over the place. The trouble was, my uncle had lived by the sea, and so although it looked all right on the outside, it was actually riddled with hidden rust. It got so bad that it developed a hole in the floor and the bolts that held the passenger seat to the floor fell out! The rust was hidden and it made the car dangerous and unsafe to drive. If I'd wanted to keep driving the car I'd have had to get someone to cut out all the rust and weld new metal in to make it sound again. Secret sin in our lives is like the rust in my old car: left unattended it grows and eventually leaves us in a state. For lots of people the only way to sort sin out, especially sin that's a secret, is to tell someone we trust about it and get them to help us sort it out. It takes huge courage to talk to someone, but it's a great way to share a burden and get help in getting things sorted. Revealing the sin and cleaning it out is painful and costly, but if we want life in all its fullness then the sin has to be sorted out.

One last thing: often when we're trying to sort sin out we become obsessed with dealing with it. Our number-one priority becomes sorting the sin, and of course that means the sin becomes our biggest focus. The best way to overcome sin in our lives is to turn round and focus on God, and you do that in worship, prayer and in reading the Bible.

REFLECT

King David might strike us as an amazing biblical character. He fought wild beasts that threatened his sheep when he was a boy, stood up to and killed the giant Goliath when a whole army were too scared to stand up to him. He remained true to God's teachings and call on his life, even when his life was being threatened by King Saul. He wrote dozens of hymns and prayers praising God – they form a good part of Psalms in the Bible – and he united the nation of Israel. In the New Testament he was remembered as 'a man after [God's] own heart' (Acts 13.22). But he was also totally human. There's a story in 2 Kings that tells of a time when King David was sitting on the roof of his palace and saw a beautiful woman in a neighbouring house. He was so struck with her that he arranged for her to be brought to his palace, and there he started an affair with her. Eventually the woman, who was called Bathsheba, falls pregnant. David tries to keep the affair a secret with lies, manipulation and ultimately by having Bathsheba's husband killed.

David, being an all-powerful king, probably thought he'd got away with it. But God reveals David's sin to the prophet Samuel and he confronts the sinful king. When he realizes how badly he's messed up, David is mortified and writes a prayer telling God how sorry he is. The prayer is recorded in the Bible as Psalm 51, and to this day has the most relevant words for helping us tell God we're sorry for what we've done.

When I've felt that I needed to ask for God's forgiveness I've done the really simple activity of taking this psalm and writing it out for myself. Saying the words is one thing, but somehow writing them helps me really to own them. If you want, you could try rewriting the psalm in your own language – try to rewrite it without using any of the words from the original text. It's a good way to help you really get your head around what the Bible might be saying.

Some people find it helpful to do something physical to demonstrate that they've confessed their sin to God and to help them realize that when we ask for forgiveness God is so quick to accept that prayer and to make us whole again. You could do something really simple like writing down your confession on a piece of paper or drawing something to represent it and then tearing the piece of paper up into tiny pieces and throwing them away. If it's safe to do so you could even burn the piece of paper so that there really is nothing left. It's a really good way to picture how God treats our confessed sin.

REACT

It's possible that you've read this passage and have that uncomfortable feeling in your gut that means you know there are things in your life that you need to get sorted. The 'react' for this chapter is quite a challenge.

You need to find an adult who you really trust, who you can talk to about what you struggle with. You may want to speak to your priest/ minister, a youth worker or another adult you respect within the church. In some churches, having a time of confession with a member of clergy is a common practice and can really help in working through ongoing sins and struggles. If no one springs to mind straight away, you might want to ask God to help you identify someone. Pray for the strength to be able to talk to that person and then to ask for help.

Remember that it's worth the discomfort to find that fullness of life that Jesus promises!

CHAPTER 7

PROCLAIM THE GOOD NEWS

DO YOU REMEMBER WHEN...
...YOU SAID YOU WOULD
PROCLAIM BY WORD AND
EXAMPLE THE GOOD NEWS
OF GOD IN CHRIST?

BISHOP PAUL:

Some people like to talk about their faith being 'private'. It is, they imply, between them and God alone. This can never square with the good news of Jesus Christ. Faith is deeply personal, yes, but it can never be simply private. Jesus sent his first disciples around Israel to tell people about the coming kingdom of God. After Jesus rose from the dead he made it very clear, time and again, that he was sending his disciples out to be witnesses to his death, resurrection and the good news of forgiveness of sins available to everyone. He was also clear that this good news was to be taken to every part of the earth. This witness was always to be both by how his disciples lived and by the message they shared.

You're a living witness for Jesus Christ, in your home, school, college, sports club, dance or drama studio. How you treat other people, how you talk to – and about – others are all part of how you share the good news by example. So sharing in acts of loving kindness, being generous with your time and money to help others, all matter. I love St Paul's image when he wrote to the Christians in Philippi, 'that you may be blameless and innocent, children of God without blemish in the midst of a crooked and twisted generation, among whom you shine as lights in the world, holding fast to the word of life' (Philippians 2.15–16 ESV). Our lives are to be like bright shining stars for others to see God's light.

Yet we also have a responsibility to speak of Jesus. The first Christians boldly spoke about Jesus' life, death and resurrection. They encouraged people to discover Jesus for themselves. As St Peter put it, 'always being prepared to make a defence to anyone who asks you for a reason for the hope that is in you; yet do it with gentleness and respect' (1 Peter 3.15–16 ESV). So Peter encourages us not to ram the gospel down people's throats or demand that they listen. He tells us to respect other people, share the good news gently and lovingly. But he does expect us to do it.

We're an outreaching people. Evangelism – telling other people about the Christian faith – is part of who we are as disciples of Jesus. We evangelize by how we live and by what and how we speak. But it's not an optional extra for some Christians, rather sharing the good news of Jesus is the responsibility of every single one of us. After all, it's the best and most exciting news the world has ever heard – so how can we possibly keep it to ourselves?!

OPENER

Have you ever heard some really good news that's totally changed your day? The kind of thing that's made you grin from ear to ear? I knew a young person who'd always wanted to be an infant-school teacher. In fact when she finished Year 2 she couldn't

> PETER [SAID], 'REPENT AND BE BAPTISED, EVERY ONE OF YOU, IN THE NAME OF JESUS CHRIST FOR THE FORGIVENESS OF YOUR SINS.' . . . ABOUT THREE THOUSAND WERE ADDED TO THEIR NUMBER THAT DAY.
>
> THEN PETER SAID, 'SILVER OR GOLD I DO NOT HAVE, BUT WHAT I DO HAVE I GIVE YOU. IN THE NAME OF JESUS CHRIST OF NAZARETH, WALK.'
> (ACTS 2.38, 41; 3.6 NIV)

understand why she had to go to another school – she'd learnt all she needed to know in order to do what she knew she wanted to do.

When it came to applying to go to university, Sophie had to get two Ds at A level in order to get on the course she'd set her heart on. She turned up at school with all of her friends to pick up her results, full of all the usual excitement, anticipation and above all nerves that we all feel on results day. Everyone got handed their envelopes and then took themselves off to somewhere away from the crowd to open them up and see whether their hard work had paid off. With the cheers and shouts of successful students ringing in her ears, Sophie tore open her envelope and looked at the piece of paper inside. It wasn't the news she'd been hoping for. She'd only managed to get a D and two E grades. That was it. All those years of dreaming and expectation were shattered. Everything she'd wanted to do since she was six years old was taken away in that one second.

At that moment the principal of Sophie's college caught her attention and beckoned her over. He'd seen her results in advance and phoned the university that had made her the offer. He'd been so convinced of her ability to become a teacher that he'd persuaded them to take her even though she hadn't got the results she needed.

Can you imagine how Sophie felt as she heard that good news? Someone believed in her enough to fight for her, to offer her a chance even though she hadn't earned it. It's an amazing story. Sophie completed her degree with good marks and is now an outstanding teacher.

Sophie's story is a great illustration of the gospel, the good news of God in Christ. At the core of the Christian faith lies the truth that not one of us is good enough to enjoy a friendship with God. Even if we try really hard we let ourselves down over and over again. The good news of the Christian faith is that the God we believe in is a truly grace–full God.

The Christian story is sometimes called the gospel or literally the good news. In every other aspect of life, success or salvation depends on what we can do or what we can offer. If you're smart enough, good looking enough or quick enough, you'll succeed. The Christian faith says that none of us could ever succeed on our own and that instead Jesus has done everything for us. He's God's Son and he's perfect. By allowing himself to be killed on the cross he made it possible for every person who's ever lived to make the grade, to be God's friend. It's an incredible story.

When I realize what God has done for me, I feel I have to tell other people. It's such good news that I can't possibly keep it to myself. I need to tell others about it!

When we think about 'proclaiming the good news' we probably think first of all about the first of the two Bible verses at the start of this chapter. We can easily picture Peter standing up in the street, speaking about what he believed as a Christian. These days we might picture someone with a big Bible standing in the street or at the front of church preaching a message. For Peter it was certainly effective. That sermon saw some 3,000 people come to faith in Jesus. It's one way of proclaiming the good news but it probably isn't the way lots of us would choose to tell others about our faith. In fact for some of us the thought of standing up and preaching the way Peter did would terrify us! I'd love to have that kind of courage, and while I quite regularly get the chance to speak in churches or in youth groups, I'm not sure I'd have the guts to do the same thing on a street corner.

I remember, in the early days of being a youth worker, I took a day off and went to London with my wife. We'd planned the usual thing

– mooching around the shops for the afternoon, grabbing something to eat and finishing the day by going to see a show. We entered a shopping mall and there was someone standing on a corner with a folder and a Bible, preaching the gospel. When we walked past him he caught us and asked us whether we'd ever thought about the Christian faith. I gave him a conspiratorial wink and said that I was actually a Christian youth worker. He asked me what we were doing for the day, and my wife explained that we were in London for a day off. At this point the man got really angry with us. 'A day off?' he shouted, 'What do you mean, a day off? Do you think Jesus ever took a day off?' He was still shouting as we literally ran out of the building!

The trouble is, his words stuck with me – I really had to question myself to try to work out whether there was an element of truth in what he'd said. Was I lazy? Was I letting Jesus down? Could I ever justify a day away from the action or should I be proclaiming the gospel, just like this man was, every single day?

As with all things in life, our model is Jesus. How did he proclaim the good news? Did he spend every day preaching on street corners, challenging people about their lifestyle and what was going to happen to them after they died? Of course he didn't! Jesus did stand up and preach sometimes – there are a few really good examples in the Bible where he stood on hillsides, or once in a boat, and spoke about God to the crowds of people who'd gathered. But that certainly wasn't how he spent most of his time. To me it feels like he spent most of his time with smaller groups of people, telling stories and sharing meals.

What's for certain is that Jesus didn't just share the gospel by what he said. He also acted in a way that meant people could know that his message was good news. So as well as talking to people about God and forgiveness and love and grace, he also cared for the sick, comforted the poor and fed the hungry. The majority of people who came to Jesus did so because they thought he might be able to heal them. St Francis summed up this approach to sharing God's love when he said, 'Preach the gospel at all times and when necessary use words.' For St Francis, the way we live and the good news we show through our actions is far more important than the words we say.

In the Bible passage from Philippians (on page 76) we see Peter proclaiming the gospel by word, but in the one from Acts (on page 77) he proclaims it by his deeds, in this case healing a lame man begging outside the temple gate.

If we think sharing the good news with people is based just on what we say to them, then I think we miss the true nature of evangelism. That's why in your confirmation the bishop was very careful to ask you whether you would proclaim the good news of Jesus Christ by word *and* example. The two go hand in hand.

I've never really thought of myself as an evangelist. I worry that I'm not brave enough. But several times in my life things have happened that have helped me to see how God is using me to share the gospel, in a really natural way. A friend of my wife's once knocked on our door in a real state because things had got on top of her in life and she knew that Kathryn and I were the kind of people who'd listen and care and love. She wanted to know where God was in her life and she knew that we'd be able to help her answer some questions.

I regularly go running with a friend who's an atheist. I rarely start conversations about the Christian faith and yet time and time again we talk about what I believe because he asks me questions. In fact he and his wife once came for dinner and we ended up talking about how there could be a God when there was so much suffering in the world. Again, the conversation was started by our guests – we didn't force it on them.

Proclaiming the good news of Jesus Christ means that people recognize something about you that causes them to ask questions about your faith. Maybe you're less quick to judge than others, or you think of other people in situations where others think only of themselves. The key is being ready to talk about your faith when people want to hear, to be able to answer questions about why you're a Christian and what that means for you. Does that get us off the hook of sometimes having to be ready to stand up and speak? Not entirely – there'll always be times when that might be what's required of us, and some people will always find that easier than others. But for the most part, proclaiming the good news of Jesus Christ means something much wider than just that picture of evangelism.

REFLECT

Not surprisingly, prayer and Bible reading are important parts of evangelism. God listens when we pray for someone who isn't a Christian, and it means that when we talk to that person about our faith we can be really confident that God will help us out with what we say and how we might reply to questions. Praying for opportunities also makes us more aware of situations where we can talk to others – it keeps us alert to what's going on around us.

You might have friends or other acquaintances you're already aware you'd like to talk to. If so, why not put a picture of them in a place where you'll regularly see it, maybe somewhere in your room or on the screensaver on your computer or phone. You could write, 'Proclaim the good news by word and example' on the photo or, if you're putting the picture on your computer or your phone, try using some kind of photo-editing software to write similar words on that picture.

Finally, if you get the chance to talk to someone about your faith – to proclaim the good news by word – it's worth having an idea of what you might say. Grab a piece of paper and a pen and answer these two questions: How did you become a Christian? What does being a Christian mean for you?

REACT

A few years ago the Church of England produced a great little pamphlet called *Love Life Live Lent*[11] that's packed full of little things that anyone could do to spread the love of God around their neighbourhood.

Ideas included:

- say something nice about someone behind their back;
- clean out your room and take anything you don't need to a charity shop;
- give up your place in a queue to someone else;
- skip a meal and give the money to a charity working overseas;
- smile at someone.

You get the idea. These indiscriminate acts of kindness are real kingdom moments. They hint at what the world could be like – will be like one day.

Why not write out a list of 30 acts of kindness and do one a day for the next month – you might just enjoy it enough to keep doing it!

SEEK AND SERVE CHRIST IN ALL PEOPLE

DO YOU REMEMBER WHEN...
...YOU SAID YOU WOULD
SEEK AND SERVE CHRIST
IN ALL PEOPLE,
LOVING YOUR NEIGHBOUR
AS YOURSELF?

BISHOP PAUL:

When I was a vicar in east London, Tony and Barry used to call at our house regularly. They wanted a cup of tea, a sandwich and a bit of a chat. We were usually more than happy to oblige. They lived close by, and for a variety of reasons lived on state benefits. They were our neighbours, who sought us out. We could serve them in this way. A sad statistic from our time in east London was that among everyone in our neighbourhood it was officially stated that more than one third of people didn't even know the names of the people living in the flats or houses immediately next to them. Their literal next-door neighbours were complete strangers.

I'm very fortunate, I have a wonderful large family and many friends. I realize this is not true for many people. It would be easy for me just to confine myself to meeting and engaging with people like me who hold the same values and ideas, people with whom I find it easy to get on and whose company I enjoy. This in reality is what many people do in life. However, Jesus calls us to seek and serve all people, not just those we like. He calls us to recognize those who disagree with us, even persecute us, as neighbours we should serve. He calls us to love the unlovely, touch the untouchable and bring hope to those in despair.

So we can love our neighbours – the ones we meet every day at school, in our street and at home – by seeking the best for them. When these are friends and family this may be relatively easy and straightforward. But we're also called to put ourselves out, to step outside our comfort zones and seek out neighbours who need friendship, love and care, even if we find it hard to offer it to them. I wonder who God might be asking you to show his love to that you'd really rather avoid?

OPENER

The story that Jesus tells about a Jewish man being rescued by a Samaritan is probably the best known of all of Jesus' parables (Luke 10.25–37). You've probably heard it hundreds of times and may even have retold it yourself. You've probably

> **'WHO IS MY NEIGHBOUR?'**
> **(LUKE 10.29 NIV)**

even heard lots of 'modern' versions of it. I worked as a youth worker in Portsmouth for a couple of years, and we used to tell the story of the Portsmouth FC supporter who was rescued by the Southampton supporter (very controversial!).

The trouble with any story that gets retold so many times is that it can easily lose its impact. We hear it start and we know it so well that we tune out and miss the rest of it.

As with most of Jesus' stories, he uses images and experiences his listeners would have been really familiar with. The road the traveller was on was a notorious 17-mile route that linked the cities of Jerusalem and Jericho. It skirted the area of Samaria, which was home to a tribe of people the Jewish people hated with a passion: the Samaritans.

The road was renowned for being a dangerous route to travel – rocky and remote, with caves and boulders along its sides. The perfect place for thieves and muggers to hide out and prey on unprotected travellers. If you want a modern-day equivalent, imagine walking through a city centre late at night by yourself. The people listening to Jesus' story would have travelled the route themselves and would probably have known of people who'd been attacked by thieves.

SEEK AND SERVE CHRIST IN ALL PEOPLE

The story says that while a man was walking along the road the worst happened: he was attacked, beaten up and robbed. The thieves left him for dead on the road and made off with his possessions.

Imagine yourself in his position, lying by the road, drifting in and out of consciousness, fearing that you're going to die. It would have been terrifying.

As he's lying there a Jewish priest comes towards him. Often when we retell this story we imagine that the priest is a bit like a modern-day vicar, and to us that makes the story rather shocking. We can't imagine any vicar passing someone by in their moment of need. It's totally outside our experience. A Hebrew priest was quite different from a modern-day vicar. He'd have served in the temple in Jerusalem, accepting sacrifices from the people and offering them to God on their behalf. The Hebrew people had a strict set of laws and rules that they stuck to, and high on that list were laws about purity. If any Jewish person touched something that was unclean, they'd have to undergo a series of cleansing rituals, including a certain amount of time out of contact with other people.

I'm certain that when the priest sees the man lying by the side of the road he must want to help him. In fact as a priest there were laws that dictated that he must help out those in need, particularly a Hebrew brother. Can you see the problem he faces? He'd have been under two conflicting laws, one commanding him to help the man out and another to remain clean. Touching the blood of the dying man, or if the man was already dead, touching his body, would have violated that law about cleanliness. And so he passes by, even crossing to the other side of the road to put as much distance between himself and the victim as possible.

Have you ever been in a situation where you've felt this kind of conflict? Maybe a friend was having a tough time at school and really wanted to talk to you, but your parents were expecting you home. On the one hand you've got a friend who needs you, and on the other you know you'll be in trouble if you're late. Sometimes it's just impossible to get it right!

When Jesus' listeners heard that the priest passed the man by, they wouldn't have been surprised – they'd have understood the conflict he was facing.

Some time later, a Levite, a man who served in the temple, comes across the man in the road. Again he takes a look at the dying man and faces the same conflict. Like the priest he decides to stick with the purity law, crossing the road and passing on by.

And then Jesus introduces a twist into the story: a Samaritan man enters the scene, walking the road with his donkey.

I don't know if you've ever been to a pantomime, but if so you'll know that whenever the baddy comes on stage everyone in the audience boos and hisses. That's probably how the people listening to Jesus' story would have reacted when Jesus introduced the Samaritan to the narrative. To say that the Jews hated the Samaritans is really understating the situation. A Jew would have viewed a Samaritan as less than human – it was a really horrible relationship.

So the people are booing and hissing, waiting for the Samaritan to pass the stricken man by, when Jesus flips that expectation on its head. Rather than have him leave the injured man as the listeners expected, Jesus makes the Samaritan the hero. He sees the man in need, comes up to him, binds his wounds, anoints him with oil to comfort him, loads him on his donkey, takes him to an inn and cares for him, even paying for his whole stay.[12]

Perhaps you can imagine the scene. The people would have been speechless. Their holy men, the priest and the Levite, had walked by when the man was in so much need, and their worst enemy, a Samaritan, had stopped and loved and cared.

Jesus turns to the listeners and asks a brilliant question: 'Which of these three do you think was a neighbour to the man who fell into the hands of robbers?' Begrudgingly the reply comes that 'The one who had mercy on him' was the true neighbour (Luke 10.36, 37 NIV).

So what's the point of the story? Again, I think that we've heard it so many times that we miss the point. We often try to say that Jesus was trying to tell us to put aside problems with enemies or love them, and although he does at other times tell people that's how he wants them to behave, I don't think that's his message here. I think his story has two messages for us. The first is very simple: when you see someone in need you should try to help them. Wow: newsflash! Sometimes we want Jesus to be saying something deep and profound, and actually what he asks his followers to do is as simple as keeping an eye out for people in need and doing something to help. The fact that the man who helped in the story is a Samaritan is almost irrelevant – Jesus just wants his followers to be the kind of people who help others out.

Jesus' second point is a little bit more profound, though. He says he wants us to be the kind of people who accept help from others, even those who we least expect would want to help us out. For lots of people the second half of this promise is much harder than the first – we might find it very easy to love other people but much more difficult to love ourselves. I come from a broken family – my dad left home when I was very young and I've never had a relationship with him. Anyone who has a similar story will know how hard it is to have a positive view of yourself when you've had that kind of experience. Part of loving yourself is accepting that other people will want to help you just as much as you might want to help them. That means allowing yourself to be vulnerable, which can be very hard. In some ways the man by the side of the road had it easy: he was in such a terrible way that he was in no position to turn down help, even from his most hated enemy. I think we have a lot to learn from him.

We're all guilty of judging other people. We see someone dressed in a certain way and we expect them to act accordingly. But Jesus says anyone can be a neighbour to anyone. It can be really hard to accept help from others. We're taught from a very young age that it's good to be independent, not to have to rely on other people. But Jesus says that when we're in need we should let people help us and shouldn't be fussy about who comes to our aid. People we think are bad, he says, are capable of doing good things, and we shouldn't be guilty of judging them before they've had a chance to show what they're capable of.

Promising to seek and serve all people and to love your neighbour as yourself is actually a pretty huge promise. You've said you'll seek and serve all people – not just the ones you like – and that you'll love your neighbour, which includes your worst enemy.

Sounds pretty heavy!

REFLECT

For this you'll need to grab a piece of paper and a pen – if you like to be creative, maybe several pens of different colours.

On the paper draw a series of five concentric circles; then label the area within each circle as shown here.

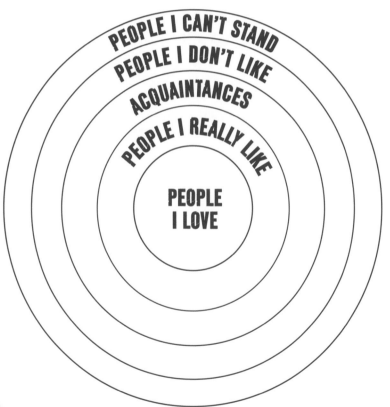

PEOPLE I CAN'T STAND

PEOPLE I DON'T LIKE

ACQUAINTANCES

PEOPLE I REALLY LIKE

PEOPLE I LOVE

Now, I'm not going to ask you to write any names down. It would be easy to fill the middle three circles, but to write down the names of people we don't like or can't stand is not a particularly healthy exercise! However, I do want you to use the circle as a way of both praying for the people you know and asking God to challenge you as you think about the people you don't like so well.

As with our other activities, you need to relax and get yourself into a place where you're comfortable and unlikely to be disturbed. You might want to read the parable of the Good Samaritan through a few times to remind yourself of what it is Jesus was teaching the people around him.

Once you're settled, start from the middle and, in your head, put the names of a couple of people into each circle. Thank God for those people, both those you love and those you can't stand. Ask God to show you how to treat people at the different levels; ask for his wisdom and his guidance. How does it feel to pray for people you don't like? Loving your neighbour as you love yourself means treating others as you'd like to be treated. What have you learnt about the way you treat others by this activity?

Perhaps you could finish your prayer by praying for yourself or asking someone else to pray for you.

Throughout its history the Christian faith is full of stories of people who've done incredible things for other people. People who've sacrificed everything for the sake of others.

Mother Teresa was a nun who lived in the Indian city of Calcutta. She gave her whole life to caring for the homeless and the orphans of that place. On the wall of her orphanage she wrote these words:

People are often unreasonable,
illogical, and self-centred;
   . . . Forgive them anyway.

If you are kind,
people may accuse you of selfish, ulterior motives;
   . . . Be kind anyway.

If you are successful,
you will win some false friends and some true enemies;
   . . . Succeed anyway.

If you are honest and frank,
people may cheat you;
   . . . Be honest and frank anyway.

What you spend years building,
someone could destroy overnight;
   . . . Build anyway.

If you find serenity and happiness,
they may be jealous;
  . . . Be happy anyway.

The good you do today,
people will often forget tomorrow;
  . . . Do good anyway.

Give the world the best you have,
and it may never be enough;
  . . . Give the world the best you've got anyway.

You see, in the final analysis,
it is between you and God;
It was never between you and them anyway.

It would be amazing to think that anyone might actually try to live out all of those actions. Maybe today you could put just one into action.

Read the list a couple of times and see if anything jumps out at you. If so, make a decision to do something about it. Imagine the difference you might be able to make to the world even just by smiling at people today – go on, change the world!

CHAPTER 9

ACKNOWLEDGE CHRIST'S AUTHORITY

DO YOU REMEMBER WHEN...
...YOU SAID YOU WOULD
ACKNOWLEDGE CHRIST'S
AUTHORITY OVER HUMAN
SOCIETY, BY PRAYER FOR THE
WORLD AND ITS LEADERS?

BISHOP PAUL:

I can't see the electricity that powers the computer on which I'm writing but I know it's real because of its effects. Every day I behave with a conviction that some things I can't see are true – like the existence of Australia, microbes, and above all God. Sometimes I even find myself accepting things contrary to some of the evidence. Acknowledging Christ's authority over human society is among these. Jesus' resurrection and then his being taken up into heaven tell us that God is triumphant over death and that ultimately all things will be brought to the conclusion that he knows what's best for all of creation. As St Paul put it:

He is the beginning, the firstborn from the dead, that in everything he might be preeminent. For in him all the fullness of God was pleased to dwell, and through him to reconcile to himself all things, whether on earth or in heaven, making peace by the blood of his cross.' (Colossians 1.18–20 RSV)

However, sometimes world leaders, and even local ones, appear to be in charge, and in particular seem sometimes to get away with some really terrible things. So I have to remind myself that in the end God is in charge, not the President of the USA or the Prime Minister or a terrorist leader. It's a problem that believers have faced throughout history – sometimes the things that are happening seem to suggest God isn't in charge, or control, or doesn't even care. As the psalmist often cried in the face of God's apparent silence or inactivity, 'How long, O Lord?' (Psalms 74, 79, for example). But God has constantly reminded his people through the prophets and then supremely through Jesus that history is in his hands, that world leaders will have to answer for what they've done and that God's love will win in the end. So I pray for world and national leaders and those who have responsibility for making big decisions in our counties, cities and local areas, that they'll have the humility to recognize that they're not in control, rather God is. I pray that they'll work for the good of everyone, especially the poor. I pray that they'll work for peace not war. I pray that they'll have wisdom to know what to do for the best and the courage to do it.

I acknowledge, accept and recognize that Jesus is Lord over all people and all things because of his triumph over death, and a conviction that one day 'every knee should bow . . . and every tongue confess that Jesus Christ is Lord, to the glory of God the Father' (Philippians 2.10–11 RSV).

OPENER

I wonder how you feel about being told what to do?

I'm pretty rubbish at taking orders. I'm the kind of person who wants full justification for anything I'm told to do. Even if it's something I want to do, I find myself really struggling, simply because I hate being told what to do.

> THEN THE ELEVEN DISCIPLES WENT TO GALILEE, TO THE MOUNTAIN WHERE JESUS HAD TOLD THEM TO GO. WHEN THEY SAW HIM, THEY WORSHIPPED HIM; BUT SOME DOUBTED. THEN JESUS CAME TO THEM AND SAID, 'ALL AUTHORITY IN HEAVEN AND ON EARTH HAS BEEN GIVEN TO ME.'
> (MATTHEW 28.16-18 NIV)

There are some people, however, who I have so much respect for that I'm happy for them to give out the orders – people I know and trust and will happily follow.

In the verses from Matthew (on the previous page), Jesus claims that he has authority over everyone and everything. No matter who or where you are, Jesus seems to be saying, I have authority over you.

Throughout the Gospels Jesus demonstrates his authority over and over again. If you're in any doubt about whether he's qualified to have this kind of worldwide authority, it might be worth considering the following stories.

JESUS HAS AUTHORITY OVER PEOPLE

I wonder if you've ever thought about how Jesus gained his disciples? It's strange that 12 men should commit themselves to following a teacher, giving up everything for him. Presumably it was a difficult life – I don't imagine there'd have been much money involved, and following Jesus certainly didn't always attract the most positive reaction from people.

Something about Jesus was just so compelling that people wanted to follow him. That's why Jesus at the beginning of Mark's Gospel can walk up to two young men fishing in a boat with their father and ask them to follow him. And without questioning they put down their nets and follow him. It's why Jesus in the next chapter in Mark can walk up to Levi, a rich and powerful tax collector, say 'Follow me' and have him respond immediately.

For these people and for so many others, Jesus has such authority that they want to follow him. It may be why you chose to get confirmed – you heard Jesus' call and you found it irresistible.

JESUS HAS AUTHORITY OVER NATURE

There's a really well-known story that appears in three of the Gospels. It tells of a time when Jesus is travelling across a lake with his disciples in a boat. He's exhausted from a busy day of preaching and healing and falls asleep in the boat. Part-way across the lake the boat hits a storm. In his version of the story, Mark (chapter 4) describes the storm as a 'furious squall', saying that the waves broke over the boat so that it was nearly swamped.

You get an idea of how bad the storm was when you remember that several of the disciples were fishermen. They made their living on the lake. They were used to storms. And yet here they are screaming for Jesus to wake up, desperate for their lives and full of disbelief at the man who sleeps in the boat, seemingly not caring if they live or die.

You also get a good idea of just how tired Jesus is – it takes a certain level of exhaustion to sleep through a storm.

Eventually the disciples manage to rouse Jesus. He stands up in the boat and rebukes the wind and the waves: 'Quiet! Be still!' he shouts, and in that moment the wind dies down and is completely calm.

Try to imagine how the disciples felt at that instant. One moment they're being thrown around in a boat, terrified for their lives, genuinely fearing that any moment they're going to sink to the depths, and then suddenly they're sitting on the lake in complete calm. If you've ever been on a rollercoaster you'll know what it's like: one minute you're being thrown around, crashing from side to side, and the next you've finished the ride and come to a halt.

'Who is this?' the disciples ask each other, 'Even the wind and the waves obey him!'

That's some authority. Our world is full of political leaders who command vast armies and have immeasurable power, but not one of them could have even the tiniest bit of influence over something so simple as the weather. Yet at Jesus' command clouds move back, the wind stops blowing and rain stops falling.

JESUS HAS AUTHORITY OVER SPIRITS

Another time, Jesus is out walking with his followers when they come across a man who the Bible says is possessed by spirits (the story is found in Mark 5 and Luke 8). This man must have made a pretty sorry sight. He was violent and out of control and people had tried all sorts of ways to subdue him, even binding him with chains. Somehow, because of the spirits that lived in him, he had superhuman strength and broke the chains he was tied with. And so he lived in the tombs away from any people and spent his time, night and day, roaming around, screaming and cutting himself.

When he sees Jesus, the man runs to him and falls on his knees before him. 'Come out of this man, you impure spirit!' Jesus shouts. At the top of his voice the man replies, 'What do you want with me, Jesus, Son of the Most High God? In God's name don't torture me!' It seems that rather than talking to the man, Jesus is actually talking to the impure spirit: 'What is your name?' Jesus asks. 'My name is Legion,' he replied, 'for we are many.'

No wonder this man's in such a state – there isn't just one spirit living in him but many. It's a scary picture that's not easy to understand.

What's reassuring is that in the face of Jesus, the demons seem to have no power. They're clearly terrified of him. Jesus, as ever, takes pity on this poor man and sends the demons out of him.

Again, it's an amazing story and an incredible demonstration of power – not only does nature submit to Christ, so does the spirit world, things outside our understanding.

JESUS HAS AUTHORITY OVER SICKNESS

Shortly after the incident with the possessed man Jesus is on his way through a town. Hearing that he's there, people have turned out in their thousands to see him, desperate to bring him their sick, touch him or hear his words.

One woman, says Mark in chapter 5, has been suffering for 12 years with her affliction of an internal bleeding that hasn't stopped in all that time. This poor woman's illness would have made her a complete social outcast. There were strict rules about cleanliness, and her bleeding would have made her an 'untouchable'. Nobody would be able to come near her because to do so would have made them unclean also. It must have been an incredibly lonely and frightening experience for her. She's spent every penny she has on doctors, trying to find a cure, and all to no avail. So desperate is she to find healing that she pushes her way through this crowd to try to get near Jesus in the hope he might make her better.

For some reason she lacks the confidence to speak to Jesus face to face – perhaps she's embarrassed by her condition, maybe she's so tired from being ill for so long or perhaps she's just too shy to want to be the focus of attention. Instead she reaches out from the press of people and just touches the edge of his cloak. Immediately, the Bible says, her bleeding stops. She's healed.

Often when Jesus heals people he says some words, or in one instance he rubs mud in the eyes of a blind man. But such is his authority that in this story it appears he doesn't even need to say or do anything. Just by touching his cloak the woman is made whole.

JESUS HAS AUTHORITY OVER DEATH

Jesus' authority isn't just restricted to the living. He even has authority over the dead.

When the woman who was bleeding had caught up with Jesus in the crowd, he'd been on his way to the house of Jairus, a synagogue leader whose daughter was dying. Jesus' delay meant that before he could get to Jairus' house the young girl had died.

Rather than giving up and going home, Jesus continues to the house and, once he's cleared the mourners out of the building, goes to where the little girl is lying, takes her by the hand and whispers, 'Little girl . . . get up'. Immediately she gets up and starts to walk around the room.

There's nothing Jesus doesn't have authority over. Nothing can stand in his way. Even his own death isn't strong enough to stop him.

It's an amazing source of comfort for us to know that Christ is in charge of all things. Regardless of what's going on around the world, we can trust that above it all Jesus has authority.

That's why its so important for us to pray for the world and it's leaders. I'll never understand how it works, but Jesus, with all his authority, says that when we pray for our world it makes a difference. He listens to what his children are saying and acts accordingly.

That means that when a political leader has a big decision to make, we should ask for God to help her, to give her the wisdom and the understanding she needs to get things right. It means that when something goes wrong in the world – a natural disaster or a war – we can pray for God to be involved, to look after people, to lessen their suffering. By asking us to pray, Jesus is putting some of that authority in our hands. As with so many parts of the Commission that you prayed at your confirmation, it's a big responsibility. Being a Christian means getting involved with the world, being part of God's plan to make things right.

REFLECT

Sometimes the most difficult part about praying for the world can be knowing where to start. You look at the news or open a newspaper and there seems to be so much to pray for. It seems so daunting that you'd be forgiven for giving up and moving on.

The Church of England publishes daily prayers that can help lead you in your intercessions (praying for others). They're published in a book called *Daily Prayer*. You can either borrow a copy from your church (maybe ask the vicar first) or if you have internet access then visit http://www.churchofengland.org/prayer-worship/join-us-in-daily-prayer.aspx. Once there you have a choice between morning prayer, evening prayer and night prayer, so just click on the relevant time of day and read through – you might be surprised by what you get out of it. If you're simply looking for some ideas of things to pray about, skip straight to the intercessions part of the liturgy and use the ideas there – you can get straight to it at http://daily.commonworship.com/prayers/cycle.html#seasonal.

If you want to take the daily-prayer thing a step further, why not see whether it's said daily at your church or a church nearby and go and join in from time to time.

Sometimes things can seem so huge that even when we know what to pray for we simply can't think of the words. In Romans, Paul writes that sometimes 'We do not know what we ought to pray for, but the Spirit himself intercedes for us through wordless groans' (8.26 NIV). The Holy Spirit lives within us and sometimes prays on our behalf. Jesus knows we can't always think of the words to use to pray but he listens to what's going on in our hearts. To him those kinds of prayers are just as important as the most carefully thought-out words.

REACT

If you want to get more involved in supporting your leaders then there are plenty of ways to do just that. There's a website called TheyWorkForYou.com. Visit the site and put your postcode into the search box – you can then find everything your local MP has talked about in parliament and can request that you get an email every time he or she speaks.

Why not use that as a way to pray for your local politicians. You could even let them know you're doing it if you like. Or you could let them know you're following them and ask them if there's any way you could get involved. Praying for our leaders means more than just interceding for them – you can put your prayers into action. If you're stuck for how to pray for our leaders, the group Christians in Parliament offers this prayer for you to use:

Lord, the God of righteousness and truth, grant to our Queen and her government, to members of Parliament and all in positions of responsibility, the guidance of your Spirit. May they never lead the nation wrongly through love of power, desire to please, or unworthy ideals; but laying aside all private interests and prejudices keep in mind their responsibility to seek to improve the condition of all mankind; so may your kingdom come and your name be hallowed. Amen.[13]

CHAPTER 10

DEFEND THE WEAK

DO YOU REMEMBER WHEN...
...YOU SAID YOU WOULD
DEFEND THE WEAK AND
SEEK PEACE AND JUSTICE?

DEFEND THE WEAK

BISHOP PAUL:

Whenever I say these words, in my mind I see children in abject poverty in nations like Burundi and Rwanda (in central Africa) whom it's been my privilege, and sadness, to see and meet. I think too of those who need protection in our world, like adults with learning difficulties, the severely disabled and runaway children. My mind goes to parts of the world where there's conflict, whether that be the Middle East, parts of Africa, Asia or closer to home.

Every time I read the Gospels I'm struck afresh by how Jesus offered healing to the unexpected in his society. He cleansed lepers, healed a woman bleeding from her womb, raised Jairus' daughter from death and welcomed being with those regarded as outcasts. He treated people in a radically different way.

So he commissions us to follow in his steps, defending the weak we know. He commissions us to be peacemakers where we are. He calls us to work for justice in our own settings. Yet as we do so we may well find ourselves drawn into being concerned for particularly vulnerable groups more widely, or passionate about a particular part of the world or issues of peace and justice around the globe.

I've been inspired by reading of Christians in the past who struggled for the abolition of slavery; better working conditions in mines, fields and factories; rights for women and children. I'm inspired today by people I meet and hear about who are working to ensure we care for our environment, working with those living with HIV & AIDS, improving education, helping child-led households, seeking to reconcile Jews and Arabs living in Israel/Palestine and much else besides.

When you were commissioned at your confirmation you were commissioned to be passionate for the needy and passionate for peace and justice. Don't be half-hearted about this – it's part of God's call on your life.

OPENER

A while ago there was a story in the news about a very wealthy celebrity who had an affair with a less well-known woman. As the man was so wealthy he was able to pay a lot of money to go to court to keep his affair a secret. The woman was unable to afford the same privilege. As a result, her photograph was splashed all over the newspapers while his identity remained secret for much longer.

> **WHAT DOES THE Lord REQUIRE OF YOU? TO ACT JUSTLY AND TO LOVE MERCY AND TO WALK HUMBLY WITH YOUR GOD.** (MICAH 6.8 NIV)

Once, Jesus was sitting in the courts of the temple in Jerusalem when the teachers of the law and the Pharisees – the religious leaders of the time – brought before him a woman who they claimed had been caught in the act of adultery. They threw the woman in front of Jesus and asked him to decide what should be done with her.

It's a bit of an odd opening to a story (which you'll find in John 8), and it teaches us a lot about the culture that Jesus lived in. For the teachers of the law and the Pharisees there was nothing more important than trying to keep the law God had given Moses in the desert after the Hebrews had been set free from the slavery in Egypt. I'm pretty sure these Pharisees were essentially good men, or at least they had good intentions. They knew the Scriptures inside out, and they knew that they taught that their people, the Hebrews, were a chosen race. They were set apart from the rest of the population of the planet and they were special in God's eyes. They also knew God had a plan for them, and central to that plan was that one day he'd send a man to save them. The trouble was that the Hebrews had been waiting for centuries for this man, the Messiah, and there seemed to be no sign of his coming.

The Pharisees were convinced that if only people could keep the laws God had set, the Messiah would come. So they made sure they studied the laws until they knew them all, and then they did everything in their power to get them exactly right.

The laws of Moses stated that adultery was a very serious crime. Any woman who was found guilty of adultery was to be brought up in front of the people and stoned to death. Pretty grim stuff. And because of the way society worked in Jesus' time, she wouldn't have been allowed to speak out for herself, for women were viewed as inferior to men. In the UK in the twenty-first century, we're working hard to iron out any inequalities between men and women, but that isn't the case elsewhere in the world even today – in some countries a woman can still be severely punished or even killed for committing adultery with a man, and the man will suffer no punishment at all.

The Pharisees in our story hoped they'd be able to catch Jesus out. They knew he loved people but they also knew he had to stick to the law. For them this seemed like a win-win situation. If Jesus told them to forgive the woman and let her go, then he'd be teaching against the law of Moses, which would prove he wasn't the Messiah. But if he agreed the woman should be killed, he'd show he was no different from any of the other teachers of the time.

If you've heard this story before then I wonder whether you've ever tried to picture what the scene must have looked like. Here is Jesus, sitting in the temple courts, surrounded by a group of shouting men and with this woman at his feet. I always imagine that Jesus remains totally calm, hardly even looking up from the ground where, the Bible says, he's quietly writing in the dust. I imagine that the teachers of the law and the Pharisees are all jostling each other, all trying to shout louder than everyone else, trying to get their questions heard, and I imagine that Jesus just remains quiet and calm. Eventually all the men fall quiet, waiting for him to say something in response to their questions. Some of them might be infuriated by his silence, others smug and self-satisfied, assuming that he has no answer.

If in your imagination you've been looking at Jesus and the men, then now you might want to let your gaze fall on the woman. Because actually this is her story – she's at the centre of it. The passage says that the teachers and the Pharisees caught her in the act of adultery (I guess I don't need to spell out what that means), so presumably she's in total disarray, her clothes in a mess, terrified for her life, sobbing and weeping. Notice also that the man she was committing adultery with is nowhere to be seen. His anonymity has been kept, and only she is being judged.

For Jesus, this scene isn't about the law, it's about this poor woman who's been dragged against her will to the temple. Jesus doesn't see a sinner or a point to be proved. Instead he sees a child of God, a woman created in God's image, one of his sisters.

Jesus really blows my mind. He just loves people so much. He's motivated by defending the weak, seeking peace and seeing justice done, just as you promised in your confirmation service. He couldn't care less about proving points and appearing to be clever. Instead he cares for people, particularly the downtrodden and poor. That's why he feeds thousands of hungry people on a hillside and touches the untouchable. It's why he cures the sick, even on a Sabbath day. For him, loving the unlovable is the most important thing he can do.

And so in the temple court, Jesus straightens up from his writing, looks around at the men and quietly says, 'Let any one of you who is without sin be the first to throw a stone at her' (John 8.7 NIV) – and then bends down again and continues to doodle in the dust.

I imagine there's silence for a moment longer and then one by one, starting with the older men, the accusers put down their rocks and slip quietly away, until only Jesus and the woman are left.

Jesus looks up again from his writing and asks where everyone has gone. 'Woman, where are they?' he says, 'Has no one condemned you?' 'No one, sir,' she says. 'Then neither do I condemn you,' Jesus declares. 'Go now and leave your life of sin' (John 8.10–11 NIV).

It really is an amazing story, one of my absolute favourites in fact. I love it because it's all about how Jesus totally changes our worldview. The men who brought the woman before him were completely caught up in their own agenda, wanted to prove a point and really didn't care who got trampled on in the process. Jesus knows the law is important but also knows there are other things even more important, such as the dignity of the poor.

His answer to the men's questions not only keeps to the word of the law but also changes the men and saves the woman. Jesus looks at the world, sees that it's filled with injustice and then says that the best way to change it is to change ourselves.

The main characters in this story are all changed, and I think we can learn something from each of them.

The men carrying the stones are changed – they go from being armed and ready to kill to quietly walking away. They'd thought they were so much better than the woman in the story, and yet when they looked at themselves they realized that in fact they were all sinners. None of them could throw a stone. It's so easy to judge other people, but much harder to take a good long look at ourselves.

It's easy to think that the woman on the ground gets away very lightly in the story, but she's changed by the encounter as well. She's broken the law and she knows she deserves punishment – her guilt isn't in question. And although Jesus saves her, he doesn't entirely let her off the hook – 'Go now and leave your life of sin,' he tells her. Do you think she changed her ways? I imagine this encounter must have changed her in some way.

Being people of peace and justice involves allowing Christ to change us. Your confirmation was a way of publicly declaring that you'd been changed and that you were continuing to be changed. If we're to defend the weak and seek peace and justice, we need to be willing to put down our stones and change the way we live. Are you up for that challenge?

REFLECT

The following is a Franciscan blessing. The words are challenging and provocative. It's one of those prayers that you don't want to say lightly in case God answers it.

May God bless you with discomfort at easy answers, half truths, and superficial relationships, so that you may live deep within your heart.

May God bless you with anger at injustice, oppression, and exploitation of people, so that you may work for justice, freedom and peace.

May God bless you with tears to shed for those who suffer from pain, rejection, starvation and war, so that you may reach out your hand to comfort them and to turn their pain into joy.

And may God bless you with enough foolishness to believe that you can make a difference in this world, so that you can do what others claim cannot be done.

As you read the words, ask God to show you where there's injustice and give you the courage to do something about it.

REACT

In Chapter 8 we made a list of indiscriminate acts of kindness that we could do to make little differences in our world. At the end of this chapter I want to challenge you to think about whether there are any much bigger changes you might want to try to make in that world.

Christians are called to be activists – we're called to look at the world, see what we don't like about it and to try to make a difference. It's all about helping to build God's Kingdom.

Here's a step-by-step plan for becoming an activist – start at the beginning and stop when you've had enough!

1. IDENTIFY YOUR PASSION

What is it that makes your blood boil? Is there anything going on in the world around you that makes you think, 'That just can't be right'?

2. CHANNEL YOUR PASSION

Develop a personal response to the issue you've identified. Write about it, paint it, blog it or Facebook it. Write poetry or a song! Whatever you do, make it a personal thing.

3. STUDY IT

Read books, blogs and websites to find out all you can about your issue. Use BibleGateway.com or a similar Bible site to see what God has to say about your issue. Ask people you know how they feel about the issue.

4. EXPLORE

The internet is a great place to get started with being an activist – you can make a difference sitting in front of your laptop! Search for organizations that are involved with your cause and find out what you can do. Who should you be emailing and petitioning? Where can you get your voice heard?

5. RECRUIT

Chat to family and friends, tell them what you think, ask how they feel, get them on board. Did you know that adults are far more likely to change their behaviour because their child has asked them to than if the government tells them?

6. SPREAD THE CAUSE!

Join an organization or, if that fails, start one so that you can talk to others who feel the same as you. If it's suitable, you could join a campaign or a demonstration. Write a blog, stories for your local paper or maybe even write a book – the sky's the limit![14]

LIVING YOUR CONFIRMATION

We want to finish this book by reminding you how it started: confirmation doesn't mark the end of a journey but is all about giving you the tools you need to continue in your life with Christ.

As Christians we're on a constant journey – we'll only reach our final destination when we meet Christ face to face. If you're willing to trust in Jesus, to listen for his voice and to seek his leadership in your life, then it will never get dull. Sometimes you'll need to go back over things, you'll need to re-learn old truths you've forgotten or strayed away from, but that's all part of continuing on the journey. We've found writing this book challenging for just those reasons: it's reminded us of things we'd forgotten and challenged us to think again about what it means to be a Christian.

What you can be certain of is that Christ promises to walk with you the whole way – he'll never leave and never give up on you (see Hebrews 13.5).

NOTES

1 *Common Worship: Christian Initiation* (London: Church House Publishing, 2006), p. 119. Copyright © The Archbishops' Council, 2006. Material from this work is reproduced by permission. All rights reserved. copyright@c-of-e.org.uk.

2 'Unction' means 'an anointing' – when the Holy Spirit is given to a Christian to mark her or him as special or 'set apart' for God.

3 http://www.churchofengland.org/prayer-worship/worship/texts/principal-services/holy-communion/preparation.aspx, accessed 23 May 2011.

4 See note 3.

5 Adapted from 'An Order for Morning Prayer', *Common Worship: Services and Prayers for the Church of England* (London: Church House Publishing, 2000), p. 31.

6 Adapted from 'Authorized Forms of Confession and Absolution', *Common Worship: Services and Prayers for the Church of England*, p. 136. Copyright © The Archbishops' Council, 2000. Material from this work is reproduced by permission. All rights reserved. copyright@c-of-e.org.uk.

7 Mark Yaconelli, *Helping Teenagers to Pray* (London: SPCK, 2009), pp. 39–40.

8 Yaconelli, *Helping Teenagers to Pray*, p. 40.

9 Taken and slightly adapted from the *Catholic Encyclopaedia* at http://www.newadvent.org/cathen/11554a.htm, accessed 24 May 2011.

10 Philip Yancey, *What's So Amazing About Grace?* (Grand Rapids, MI: Zondervan, 2002), p. 70.

11 *Love Life Live Lent: Transform Your World* (London: Church House Publishing, 2008). Available in several versions, with online support at http://www.livelent.net.
12 For further commentary on the parable in Luke, see http://www.biblegateway.com/resources/commentaries/ IVP-NT/Luke/Discipleship-Looking-Our-Jesus.
13 http://www.christiansinparliament.org.uk/prayer/ prayersfortheparliament/tabid/142/Default.aspx.
14 This list is taken in part from http://www.dosomething.org/ actnow/actionguide/become-activist, accessed 17 February 2011.